Poetry Works P...
TEACHER NOTES
1

David Harmer

Ann Tregenza

Contents

*These **Poetry Works** Posters Teacher Notes are split into two halves. Part 1 guides you through all the features of the poems and provides some stimulating activities for the classroom. Part 2 shows how the range of poems can be used to fulfil objectives from The National Literacy Strategy for England at text, sentence and word levels.*

PART 1	Introduction	3	PART 2		Introduction	39
	Wind	4	Term 1		Wind	40
	Song	6			Song	42
	What is Sharp?	8			What is Sharp?	44
	Nature Shapes	10			Nature Shapes	46
	Weather Band	12			Weather Band	48
	Fish	14			Fish	50
	Crescent Moon	14			Crescent Moon	50
	Up the Stairs to Bed!	15			Up the Stairs to Bed!	52
	Animal Sneezes	16			Animal Sneezes	53
	Caribbean	17	Term 2		Caribbean	54
	Chinese New Year in China Town	19			Chinese New Year in China Town	56
	Diwali	21			Diwali	58
	Moonwatcher	24	Term 3		Moonwatcher	60
	Flu	26			Flu	62
	Bubble Trouble	27			Bubble Trouble	64
	Says of the Week	28			Says of the Week	66
	Full and Empty	30			Full and Empty	68
	Eyes Bigger Than …	32			Eyes Bigger Than …	70
	It's Not Fair	33			It's Not Fair	72
	Feet	33			Feet	74
	The Wise Young Owl	35			The Wise Young Owl	76
	A Shaggy Dog Story	37			A Shaggy Dog Story	78
			Glossary			79

Acknowledgements

Many thanks to all the poets for contributing their work to this publication.
'What is Sharp?' © 1999 John Foster, included by permission of the author.
'Says of the Week' © 1991 John Foster from *Four o'clock Friday* (Oxford University Press), included by permission of the author.

Folens books are protected by international copyright laws. All rights are reserved. The copyright of all materials in this book, except where otherwise stated, remains the property of the publisher and authors. No part of this publication may be reproduced, stored in a retrieval system, or transmitted, in any form or by any means, for whatever purpose, without the written permission of Folens Limited.

David Harmer and Ann Tregenza hereby assert their moral rights to be identified as the authors of this work in accordance with the Copyright, Designs and Patents Act 1988.

Editor: Nancy Terry   Layout artist: Philippa Jarvis
Cover design: Martin Cross

© 1999 Folens Limited, on behalf of the authors.

Objectives from *The National Literacy Strategy, Framework for Teaching*, published by the DFEE.

First published 1999 by Folens Limited, Dunstable and Dublin.
Folens Limited, Albert House, Apex Business Centre, Boscombe Road, Dunstable, LU5 4RL, United Kingdom.
ISBN 184163 377–1
Printed in the United Kingdom by Ashford Colour Press.

PART ONE
Introduction

This collection of poems is aimed at the non-specialist teacher who would appreciate some support when delivering a wide range of genres of poetry. The intention is to provide poems that are accessible, refreshing, contemporary and written by poets experienced in producing work for children. As well as a broad range of genres this collection features a good gender mix of poets.

Each poster is accompanied by a set of teacher's notes which explain how the poem works technically. The level of detail is not aimed at children, but to inform teachers of what is happening inside each poem and what techniques the poet has employed to achieve the intended effect. Various elements of each poem, the rhyming scheme, the rhythmic structures and the images and vocabulary the poem uses are explored in a straightforward and lively manner. Many technical terms are fully explained and appear in bold type. They are then defined both in the text and in a glossary. The notes also contain well tested activities for teachers to use with their class; activities that will develop the children's understanding and enjoyment of poetry and, hopefully, interest and excite them to produce poetry of their own.

For those of you who are using the pupil text books in this series we have also included a section, where appropriate, which suggests activities that link the teacher-led lessons to the pupils' independent work.

Children respond with energy and enthusiasm to good poetry. They are captured by the beat and rhyme, the humour and the zest of poems. They enjoy hearing a broad mix of styles and forms when poems are read to them. They love to read, write and perform poetry and will find many stimulating poems in this collection to help them enhance their skills. Other poems within the collection respond to the quieter, more serious side of experience, challenging children to think about their lives and the world they inhabit. The collection is crammed with funny poems, rhyming poems, serious poems, long poems, short poems, non-rhyming poems, delicate imagistic poems and big fat beefy poems.

Using Poetry Works, children will develop and capture a sense of poetry, a sense of what a poem is and how they can make one for themselves. This collection aims to foster an excitement about poetry, it aims to pass on technical know-how that will enable children to structure their work and develop it beyond the mundane. Most importantly, it aims to let children and the people who teach them enjoy themselves.

Wind *by Andrew Collett*

About the poem

This poem is a simple and **regular rhyming** poem. It is in three stanzas of four lines each.

About the poet

Andrew Collett was born in Cleethorpes in 1963. A frustrated teacher who could not find enough suitable poetry material, Andrew decided to write some of his own. Since then he has had well over one hundred poems published. Andrew now writes and performs his poetry in schools across the country.

Rhyme

The poem rhymes the second and fourth line of each verse. This can be written abcb defe ghih. In addition, Andrew Collett uses the occasional **internal rhyme**, for example, in stanza two, line two, he rhymes *creak* with *tree* and links this with the fourth line that ends with *sea*.

Wind

It pulls at your clothes
it tugs at your hair,
it whispers on windows
to make people stare.

It rattles your rooftop
it creaks past each tree
it charges down chimneys
and roars with the sea.

It climbs with each cloud
it dives down below,
for the wind is with you
wherever you go.

Andrew Collett

Rhythm

The poem has a strong, regular rhythm which is helped along by the mainly one-syllable rhymes confirming its beat. This thumping rhythm represents the strength of the wind beating against clothing, hair, windows ... The poet is using form and structure to link directly with meaning. The powerful verbs at the start of the poem (*pull* and *tug*) set the tone and carry the poem along by their rhythm.

Personification

The poet is giving the wind a personality – a voice which *whispers* and *roars*, and has an ability to move in an animal or human way. It can *climb*, *dive*, *charge*, *pull* and *tug*. This gives the poem a real immediacy for the reader or listener because they will recognise and understand those actions. The wind is portrayed as a living thing, another device giving energy and zest to the poem.

Alliteration

The device of **alliteration** refers to the repetition of initial letters within a line. Good examples can be found in *it whispers on windows, It rattles your rooftop* and *it charges down chimneys*. This device draws each line together and adds a further energy to the already strong rhythm. There are other examples in the final verse, where again the beat of the line is further emphasised. In this stanza, the compactness of the alliterative rhythm is echoed by the deliberate contrast between the first two lines: *It climbs with each cloud, it dives down below*. We can see the wind climbing and swooping like some giant bird. Again, Andrew Collett confirms meaning with the form of the poem and the devices he uses to control that form.

Suggested activities

1. Compile a class list of movement and sound verbs that could be applied to the wind and how it affects everyone. You might suggest words like 'snatch', 'throw', 'toss', 'fling', 'grab', 'howl' and 'scream'. Then use Andrew Collett's poem as a frame and substitute the new verbs. You might also extend this activity to other types of weather. The children could write a poem called 'Rain' or 'Sunshine' or 'Snow' using the same framework, but changing the verbs. This activity links the poems to the idea of observation. The poet's observation of the action of the wind and its effects is very accurate. It is this accuracy that will enhance the children's poems and stop them sounding mundane. As the activity develops, you may wish to experiment with different nouns in different places, as well as playing with the verbs. You could, however, keep the same idea of movement.

   The poem gradually widens its perspective from verse one, which is about people, to include the wind's effect on the whole world and its living things. In these activities, it would be wise to avoid rhyme, unless it occurs naturally, but to keep the regular pattern of three verses of four lines each.

2. The children could write short poems to develop the idea of the wind as an animal. A start line such as 'The wind roared like a lion' might help, and could lead into a discussion on **simile** and the power of such simple comparisons. The whole poem could be a simile poem, for example:

   The wind roared like a lion
   Jumped like a flea,
   Hissed like a snake
   and buzzed like a bee.

3. Playing with the idea of alliteration, see how many lines the class can construct where the initial letter is repeated in as many of the words as possible. You might offer some opening ideas, for example, 'Where the wicked wind was, worried the Western wizard witless'. Each line should have a different initial letter, and the challenge is not only to think of the words for each line but somehow to make a fairly sensible poem out of them all!

Song *by Mary Green*

About the poem

This poem is constructed in a very regular pattern. It begins with the title and a space, then continues with a **rhyming couplet**, space, single line which rhymes with the **couplet**, space, couplet, space, single line which rhymes with the couplet, space, and so on. This very precision gives strength to the poem's structure and impact.

About the poet

Mary Green lives and works in London as a freelance writer and children's poet. She was an English teacher and Head of Special Educational Needs at Holland Park School. She also taught in primary schools.

Rhyme

The poem has a pattern that repeats three rhymes in a row which can be written as aa a bb b cc c dd d. In addition, the poet has included **internal rhymes** which add to the sing-song quality of the poem and contribute to its **cadence**.

Song

march ringing ting-a-linging
bird winging green swinging

spring singing

sun daisy corn hazy
cloud gazey june lazy

summer crazy

leaf turning summer yearning
ghost twirling red curling

autumn swirling

snowy ruffle icy bluffle
cold snuffle warm duffle

winter muffle

Mary Green

Rhythm

Mary Green uses blank spaces to slow the poem down so that the first two-line verse swings along, helped by five internal rhymes (the repeated 'ing' sound), then pauses for breath and summarises with the shorter and punchier line (that has three internal rhymes). When the poem turns to summer, the rhythms are slowed by the *daisy, hazy, gazey, lazy* rhymes, conjuring up images of rest, heat and relaxation. After the space, the rhythms pick up speed again with longer beats that lock into a very sensitive section, as summer dies and its ghost, autumn, appears. The poem then thumps into thick 'uffle' rhymes, with rather lumpy rhythms that generate a picture of everyone stamping around to get their feet warm.

Suggested activities

1 Use the four seasons to build a simple, short poem. This could be done as a class: as you call out a season, the children respond with a word or a phrase. A model might go as follows:

Winter is ... (snow, when I feel cold)
Spring is ... (green, when the buds peep out)
Summer is ...
Autumn is ...

2 Children will find it a challenge to create successful rhymes with meaning, but it might help to offer a frame that replicates the poem's end rhyme pattern. This will be the case especially if a similar theme is used and you limit the number of lines the children write. You might begin:

Deep snow lies in heaps,
The wind ... (leaps/creeps/keeps/seeps/sleeps)
and the snowman ... (use another word from the list above)

or

In the summer's heat,
Combines crop the ...
To a chugging ...

These are simple examples, but the possibilities are endless for three- or four-line poems with a rhyming pattern of aaa or aa bb. Once the children begin to see the idea, the work can be extended and the rhyming scheme made more adventurous, as long as the poem still makes sense.

You might develop these ideas further so that emphasis on the end rhyme is lessened, and emphasis on the internal rhymes and **similes** is extended, for example:

Deep snow lies in heaps like ...
The wind leaps like ...
The snowmen ...

3 Provide a frame that replicates the pattern of the poem, but instead ask the children to write **free verse** which doesn't rhyme (or if it does, it does so infrequently or by accident). They could write as many verses as are required. You might give the first or last word of each line to get the children started.

4 Point out the power of the verbs in *Song*. Suggest the children write a similar poem but use other verbs. Ask, 'What else can leaves do apart from twirl and curl? They can drop, twist, redden, burn, float, spiral ... ' Take a section of the poem and rewrite it with the new verbs before extending the idea into a fresh poem of the children's own making.

Links to the pupil text

You might link the poetry writing the children are doing with the poem about the seasons in the Pupil Book. Reiterate the importance of choosing words carefully and appropriately.

What is Sharp? by John Foster

About the poem

The poem is a simple three-stanza rhyming poem in which each stanza has four lines. The poem is essentially a **list poem** in which the meaning, suggested by the title, is explored through a variety of examples. These examples are pictures in words, or images, which bring to mind the quality of sharpness and answer the question in the title. The poem, therefore, has no real **narrative** – it doesn't move forwards in time, tell a story or develop a meaning. It expands upon one idea by giving rich and varied images that all echo each other. This list adds up to an answer. Some of the images are homely and part of everyday experience, *The point of a thorn* and *A nettle's sting*. Others are fabulous and strange but are still part of the repertoire of myths and stories familiar to young children. Look at, for example, *A witch's grin*. The apparent simplicity of the form gives the poem a great strength.

About the poet

John Foster taught English for over 20 years and is now a full-time writer. He also edits poetry anthologies and writes information books and textbooks. His hobbies are swimming and skiing and he is a keen supporter of Carlisle United. He and his wife live in Oxfordshire.

Rhyme

John Foster uses the same rhyme for the first two verses and changes it in the third. The rhyme can be written as abcb dbeb fghg. To be really accurate, *pin* and *sting* in stanza one are not full rhymes. However, their sound chimes well and is appropriate to the meaning of the poem. This device is called **near rhyme**. These rhymes help bind the poem together and reinforce its rhythm.

Rhythm

The rhythm of the poem is short and jabbing. Most lines end on a single syllable which emphasises the punchy quality of the rhythm. The poet is deliberately using form to reinforce meaning. All the rhymes, except for one, are **end-stopped rhymes**, which means that the meaning stops where they do, and John Foster reinforces this with a full stop. Not only does the line end, but the meaning and the punctuation do as well – a very spiky device! In the third line of the second verse, however, the poet lets the meaning flow round the line and carry on into the next one. This is called **enjambement** or a **run-on line** and is used to promote the flow and speed of the rhythm.

Suggested activities

1. This poem provides an ideal framework for the children to explore other 'qualities'. They can make list poems answering questions like 'What is soft?', 'What is wet?', 'What is hot?', 'What is gooey?', and so on. You might move on to suggest they investigate and write poems about less tangible and more abstract ideas, such as 'What is brave?', 'What is fear?' In these poems, the images they use should grow in complexity and it might help for you to provide an example:

What is fear?
Fear is dark.
Fear is being alone.
Fear is something I cannot see hiding in the woods.
Fear is brown and dark blue.
Fear is a scream.
Fear is a tingling skin.

These images explore more abstract ideas: the colour of fear, the sound of fear, the feel of fear. Clearly, there are lots of emotions, some positive and some less so, which can be explored.

2. Taking the idea of the list poem, ask the children to write poems that are simple lists of things they see, hear and know about around them. They might write a poem about their journey to school, including not only the physical world they experience but also the imaginative one, too. This would include their fears, hopes and daydreams as they make their journey. They might also include other characters, such as parents, older or younger siblings, or a teacher or other school personality like the caretaker. In their list poem, one line could fantasise about how those adults could change, perhaps becoming monsters or shrinking to the size of children.

The possibilities of list poems are endless. They have just one rule – that each line is an idea, an image. They teach very well both the difficult idea that poetry is written in lines and also the idea of image-building. Children will be able to compose quite complex poetry, simply by using John Foster's straightforward example.

Links to the pupil text

You might link the children's 'experience' poems with the poetry presentation in the Pupil Book. How might they present their poem so an audience understands how they feel? What tones and expressions would they use?

Nature Shapes by Sue Cowling

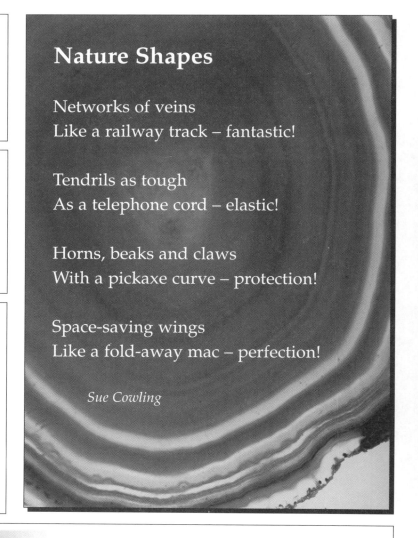

Nature Shapes

Networks of veins
Like a railway track – fantastic!

Tendrils as tough
As a telephone cord – elastic!

Horns, beaks and claws
With a pickaxe curve – protection!

Space-saving wings
Like a fold-away mac – perfection!

Sue Cowling

About the poem

This is a **regular rhyming** poem made of four pairs of lines, or **couplets**, each one of which extends into using three-syllable words in the second line.

About the poet

Sue Cowling lives near Birmingham and was a teacher. She wrote her first poem when she was nine and still prefers children's poems to grown-up ones!

Rhyme

The rhymes of the poem are simple. The last word of the first two couplets rhyme and the last word of the second two rhyme. This can be written as ab cb de fe. There is also a rhyme between the first and last verses where *track* rhymes with *mac* which binds the poem together as we hear the last couplet chime with the first.

Rhythm

Each couplet begins with a four-syllable line and ends, mainly, in a five- or six-syllable line (the last word is not included in the couplets). The exclamation marks at the end of the regular rhyming extension give a powerful kick to the line, especially as the last words are separated from the body of the line by a dash. This is where the poet links form to meaning. The couplets begin with an observation of natural images, expressed in exciting language. They are followed by the poet's comments. The poet is filled with exuberance and delight at the complexity of each, apparently simple, natural object being discussed. Observation moves to judgement with the minimum of fuss. The poem is neat and tight, expressing colourful images with economy and strength.

Links to the pupil text

You might like to extend the work on **similes** the children do in the Pupil Book by writing a fantastical class poem using crazy similes. The children will enjoy thinking up wild and extraordinary comparisons!

Imagery

Within the small space of the poem, Sue Cowling uses some very expressive images that work as simple comparisons, known as similes. These work by the use of the words *like* and *as*, where the poem gains power by unusual juxtapositions; *tendrils* are *as tough as a telephone cord* and, remarkably, *wings* are *like a fold-away mac*. The first verse brings to mind the branches of winter trees silhouetted against the sunset, or of leaves in summer. The second evokes the idea of roots or climbing plants like a Virginia Creeper. The third is the animal world, made dangerous and predatory with the strength and cruelty of the *pickaxe curve*. The fourth just has to be a bat! The poet seems to cover a vast imaginative territory, evoking the whole natural world, in a very short space and with very precise observation.

Suggested activities

1. This poem provides an ideal opportunity to teach the idea of similes. The children list their own similes, perhaps using a more obvious theme than that of the natural world. The best theme is their immediate environment – the classroom or the school grounds. This would be a good activity to perform after a walk around the locality or during a visit elsewhere. The structure of the poem, with its characteristic exclamations, would form an excellent frame on which to model the children's own poems. The first line of the model is the object of the simile, the second line the simile itself followed by an exclamation. You might offer an example:

   The blackboard
   Like a night sky – fantastic!

   My pencil
   Like a snowman's finger – just great!

   Once again, it is better to avoid rhyme unless it fits well with the meaning, although the frame produced for the children could already have the rhyming exclamations put in as:

   _____

   _____ – fantastic!

   _____

   _____ – elastic!

   Of course, the meaning of the poem would have to be maintained, so the second of the above verses would have to be something that really was stretchy!

2. Use each of Sue Cowling's couplets as the starting point for a whole poem, perhaps a class poem, which develops the theme of the first couplet as opposed to the pattern of *Nature Shapes* as a whole. The first poem, for instance, would be about trees, or leaves, or aspects of the seasons, or whatever the class decides the meaning of the couplet is. Then more lines are added to develop that point, for example:

   Networks of veins
   Like a railway track – fantastic!
   Black branches against the sky
   Bare trees, no leaves at all.
   The birds follow each line of the track
   To sing winter songs
   In the evening.

   In this way, Sue Cowling's single poem can be used to generate four freestanding poems, plus a great deal of discussion on similes and how important they are in the writing of poetry.

Weather Band *by Celia Warren*

About the poem

This poem, composed of four **couplets**, is in **free verse**. This means that it has no regular **metrical pattern** and so will not scan, although it has a tight, recognisable rhythm and beat. It doesn't rhyme in a regular way, but there are some full rhymes and there are **near rhymes** and **assonance** binding words and lines together.

About the poet

Celia Warren was born in North Lincolnshire and lives in Staffordshire. When she writes something new she drafts it first and then tucks it away for a few days. When she comes back to it she polishes the words till they shine. If the poem sounds good when she reads it out loud then it is finished. She also enjoys visiting schools and helping children to write their own poems and stories.

Weather Band

Wind is a piccolo
whistling at the window.

Thunder is a big drum
thumping at the door.

Rain is a banjo
rapping at the keyhole.

Hail is a tambourine
rattling on the floor.

Celia Warren

Rhyme

Although there is no regular pattern to the rhyme, the opening couplet rhymes the end words (*window* and *piccolo*), and the second verse rhymes with the last line (door and floor). These one-syllable **end-stops** help to confirm the lively beat of the poem. The poem uses assonance, which is when the vowel sounds within words rhyme, to bind the lines together. A good example is in the first verse where *Wind, piccolo, whistling* and *window* all echo each other internally. The opening words of each second line are **onomatopoeic** – that is, they contain a sound associated with their meaning. This adds to the beat, the rhyme and the musicality of the poem so that its meaning is evoked – that there is a band playing, as suggested by the title.

Rhythm

The poem thumps along at a brisk pace, an effect helped by using a regular, two-syllable participle as the first word of each second line. The pace of the lines is also helped by the use of **alliteration**, both within a line, as with *whistling at the window*, and between lines. The first word of each line in the first three verses begins with the same letters: *Wind* and *whistling*, *Thunder* and *thumping* and *Rain* and *rapping*. The three-syllable *piccolo* in verse one is mirrored by *tambourine* in verse four, and the two-syllable *big drum* in verse two is echoed by *keyhole* in verse three.

Imagery

Whereas Sue Cowling's poem, *Nature Shapes*, used a lot of **similes** or imagistic comparisons to make its point, Celia Warren's poem uses **metaphors**. These are far stronger comparisons because the thing described is not simply being compared with something else to evoke a response or a connection in the reader's mind, that thing now *is* something else. The wind isn't like a piccolo, the wind *is* a piccolo. Rain isn't simply like a banjo, rain *is* a banjo. All the way through the poem, the instruments themselves are present; just as the title says they will be.

Suggested activities

1. Using the poem as a model, the children can expand the range of metaphors from musical ones to, for example, animals. Perhaps the wind is a lion that is roaring at the window and the thunder is an elephant trumpeting at the door. This idea could be developed so the children come up with metaphors taken from other sources, such as mechanical objects and vehicles, but still using the appropriate verbs. Now the wind could be a hammer pounding at the window and the thunder a digger biting at the door. Some children will be able to see that mixing the metaphors of one with the verbs of another (the hammer roared, the digger howled, for example) produces even more powerful results.

   You might extend this so that the children explore themes based upon classwork in other curriculum areas. By doing this, they will begin to understand the power of metaphor and appreciate that it is one of the most fundamental characteristics of poetry.

2. Staying with the theme of weather, the children could invent a band for calmer, sunnier weather. Wind, thunder, rain and hail could be exchanged for breezes, sunshine, blue skies and heatwaves. The poem would explore other instruments with appropriate verbs to contrast deliberately with the fast and furious mood of Celia Warren's poem. This, in turn, could move on to another band that played music about snow, ice, frost and fog.

3. *Weather Band* would be an excellent **performance piece** as it could be accompanied by percussion and arranged either for several voices or for the whole class. A group could take each verse in turn, for example, or a small group of children could be responsible for orchestrating and performing the whole thing. Once the groups are familiar with the words, you might try the poem as a round – a very effective idea!

Fish by Ruth Underhill
and Crescent Moon by Sue Cowling

About the poems

Both poems use the shape of words and the text itself to give a visual picture of the poem's subject. This is especially true of *Fish* which is a **calligrammic, concrete poem**. The poem physically looks like a fish, with the **narrative** of the fish catching the worm forming the body of the poem. *Fish* also uses the device of **alliteration** and the words *splish* and *splash* are examples of **onomatopoeia**.

Crescent Moon has a conventional first line but the second line, *The silver hook*, curves like the crescent moon itself. This gives the poem a visual impact to match its meaning.

About the poets

Ruth Underhill worked in the travel industry before qualifying as a nursery nurse. Since returning to England two years ago from five years in Portugal, Ruth has concentrated on writing poetry and prose for children.

For information about Sue Cowling see *Moonwatcher*, page 24.

Suggested activities

1. *Fish* shows a model concrete poem, an idea that can be expanded into many areas by the children. Make sure they understand that the words draw the picture of the subject of the poem. Houses, school, fireworks, people, vehicles, football pitches, animals, rockets, spaceships, and landscapes all make good subjects.

2. *Crescent Moon* is a poem where only part of the poem actually 'draws' the subject. Again, many themes suggest themselves, for example, the theme of a haunted house could have a line suddenly jumping up and down because it had been scared.

Up the Stairs to Bed! *by Ian Souter*

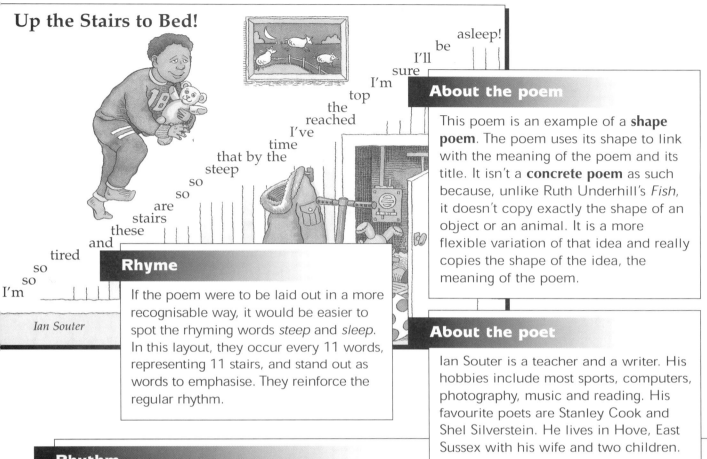

About the poem

This poem is an example of a **shape poem**. The poem uses its shape to link with the meaning of the poem and its title. It isn't a **concrete poem** as such because, unlike Ruth Underhill's *Fish*, it doesn't copy exactly the shape of an object or an animal. It is a more flexible variation of that idea and really copies the shape of the idea, the meaning of the poem.

Rhyme

If the poem were to be laid out in a more recognisable way, it would be easier to spot the rhyming words *steep* and *sleep*. In this layout, they occur every 11 words, representing 11 stairs, and stand out as words to emphasise. They reinforce the regular rhythm.

About the poet

Ian Souter is a teacher and a writer. His hobbies include most sports, computers, photography, music and reading. His favourite poets are Stanley Cook and Shel Silverstein. He lives in Hove, East Sussex with his wife and two children.

Rhythm

Again, if the poem were to be rearranged into a more conventional format, it would be easier to see that it is rhythmically quite regular. The poem starts slowly with *so so tired* as the child begins the weary hike up the stairs. It picks up speed until the pace is changed again when the words *so so* slow the poem down.

Suggested activities

1. Having considered how the poem works on the page, the children can devise other shape poems to fit the same title. They might use the actual text of Ian Souter's poem, their own, or both. They could, for example, write the poem in the shape of a bed, or as a yawn emerging from an enormous mouth.

Links to the pupil text

You might like to link this work with the work the children are doing in the Pupil Book making a poster. How might the children present the poems they have written on a poster? They might like to use a word processor to develop their writing by using different fonts and layouts.

Animal Sneezes *by Roger Stevens*

About the poem

This poem is a **calligram**, like Ruth Underhill's *Fish*, as it uses the style and size of the font to emphasise its meaning. It is also very funny!

About the poet

Roger Stevens trained as a fine artist and taught art and technology in secondary schools before moving into junior education. He now teaches part-time in Nottingham, writes and devises and delivers workshops which combine several aspects of creative writing, poetry and music. He also plays in a rock band.

Links to the pupil text

You might like to link the first activity with the work on making a class collection of animal poems in the Pupil Book by using the children's poems as part of a class display, together with the animal poem collection. Alternatively, you might like to make a class anthology of animal **shape poems**.

Suggested activities

1. Using this poem as a model, suggest the children make other poems exploiting the size of words. They could stick with the idea of animals sneezing and continue the poem, perhaps showing how a giraffe sneezes (presumably in a long, thin, stretchy way) or how an octopus sneezes (eight times at once).

   This activity can then be extended into making poems of other animal noises, exploiting the size and shape of letters to show, for example, a cow's moo or a cat's purr.

2. Roger Stevens' poem, or any poems like this that the children create, make great **performance pieces** with the size of the letters dictating volume and pace. This could be extended into producing individual or class poems about traffic noise, or poems about a busy street, a busy playground, the fair, the market, seaside holidays, a ghost story, or anything that requires sound. The words could be printed out using a word processor to make the most of different type sizes and characteristics. How the poems are typed or written out would act as signals for how to perform them.

Caribbean *by Anita Marie Sackett*

About the poem

The main feature of this poem is that it is an **acrostic**. This is a poem where the first letter of each line can be read downwards to form a word linked with the poem – in this case it is the same word as the title. The poem is a celebration of Caribbean culture, listing many of its unique and exotic features in an accessible and lively way. The poem is a list of images, or a set of snapshots, that add up to a whole picture, bringing to the reader the sounds, sights, traditions and delights of the Caribbean.

About the poet

Anita Marie Sackett has taught for over 25 years in primary and secondary schools in England, New Zealand and Jamaica. She enjoys all sports and has played hockey for the Jamaican National Team. She enjoys sharing her enthusiasm for poetry and gives poetry performances to both adults and children. She now lives in Essex.

Caribbean

Coral reef and carnival,
Anancy, trickster spider man,
Reggae, rap to sunsplash beat,
Ice cone syrup, juicy sweet,
Breadfruit fried, tasty dish,
Blue mountain and flying fish.
Emerald sea, blazing noon,
At Christmas poinsettia bloom.
Night time, come the mango moon.

Anita Marie Sackett

Rhyme

The poem has a strong, irregular rhyming scheme built mainly around the ends of lines. Lines seven and eight are an example of **assonance**, where the internal vowels rhyme but not all the consonants do.

Rhythm

Although the poem does not have a strictly **metrical** count, each line has either six, seven or eight syllables, so the beat is kept tight and the lines are short. This gives the poem a lively pace that emphasises the images it brings to life.

Imagery

The poem is a straightforward list of pictures from Caribbean life. It opens with contrasting images of peaceful seas and busy carnivals, then it moves on to a reference to a well-known Caribbean legend. It continues through contemporary music, with the delightful invention *sunsplash* evoking exactly the music's vibrancy and mood. It then deals with a variety of wonderful-sounding food. The poem comes to rest with less active images of Christmas and night time, ending in calm and tranquillity. In the last line, *mango moon* is a simple example of a **metaphor**, which directly compares the moon to the colour and shape of the mango, itself a Caribbean fruit.

Suggested activities

1. Children always have fun with acrostics of any type, perhaps using the letters of their first name, or a particular festival or celebration like Christmas or Diwali. It is a challenge to make the line start with the right letter and make sense. However, after a while, this form can become a cliched response to everything and should be used sparingly.

2. Using the style of Anita Marie Sackett's poem, the children could write a poem about the area in which they live. You might like to introduce the device of setting up contrasts within one line. Not every line need do this but it can be effective. For instance, loud and busy places, such as bus stations, markets and school yards can be contrasted with quieter images of water, Sunday mornings, small shops, back gardens and open countryside. The rule of this activity is that every line should contain images giving information about the area described and that the sights, smells, sounds and characteristics of the area must all be included within nine to twelve lines. It is a good idea to set a line limit for this activity to prevent it going on too long.

3. The children might write much smaller poems as postcards, perhaps of only two to three lines. In these, they could encapsulate an aspect of an area, town, school or home. Again, you can add pace by deliberately introducing the idea of contrasts within and between the lines, for example:

Our House
Crying baby, snoozing dad,
My big brother playing rock music,
Blue wallpaper, lots of flowers,
Washing drying in a windy garden.

Links to the pupil text

You might like to link the work in activity 2 with the work in the Pupil Book on feelings. The children might read aloud one of their poems to the class and discuss the emotions and feelings engendered.

Chinese New Year in China Town

by Andrew Collett

About the poem

The poem is in four stanzas, each of four lines. It has both a regular rhythm and a **regular rhyming** scheme. To reinforce its meaning, the poem begins and ends with the same two lines and with the same rhymes. It is celebrating the Chinese New Year, which begins on the first day of the new moon in February or March. The poem evokes, in simple and clear language, the excitement of the fireworks and the great procession that celebrates the festival. We see and hear the fun and happiness in the crowd and meet the giant dragons, made of bamboo and covered with brightly painted paper or silk, that lead the processions.

About the poet

Andrew Collett was born in Cleethorpes in 1963. A frustrated teacher who could not find enough suitable poetry material, Andrew decided to write some of his own. Since then he has had well over one hundred poems published. Andrew now writes and performs his poetry in schools across the country.

Chinese New Year in China Town

It's New Year's Day
in China Town,
another year
is counted down.

Fireworks shoot
showers of light
lanterns wave,
burning bright.

Children dance
in the crowd,
smiling faces
cheer out loud.

Dragons twist
up and down,
for it's New Year's Day
in China Town.

Andrew Collett

Rhyme

The poem rhymes every second line and uses the same rhyme twice in the opening and closing stanzas. This reinforces the meaning of the poem and tightens up the rhythm. The rhyming scheme of the poem is, therefore, abcb defe ghih jbkb. The rhymes in the third verse **half-rhyme** with the rhymes in the first and last verses with *crowd* and *loud*, and *down* and *town*. All sharpen the poem's bouncy rhythms.

Rhythm

The short lines, ranging from three to five syllables, give the poem a jaunty, dancing beat which echoes the theme of the poem. The rhythm is regular and takes the reader through the whole poem at a brisk pace. There is the occasional use of **alliteration**, for example, in the second stanza *burning bright*.

Suggested activities

1 Suggest the children carry out some research into Chinese New Year and its traditions by using reference books or ICT. They can then write their own poems that celebrate the festival. Using the same four-line stanza as a framework, they could list the features of the festival and describe them in terms of the light, heat and warmth of the occasion. If they use short, stabbing lines, as in *Chinese New Year in China Town*, they will retain the same sense of liveliness and fun, the feeling of dance and excitement. This is a good point at which to refer to work done on **similes** as they describe the fireworks, the crowds, the noise and bustle, and the dragon dancing. Remind the children that the right comparisons will add a lot to the meaning.

2 Now suggest the children investigate other festivals, for example, St Patrick's Day, the Notting Hill Carnival, Diwali, and so on. How did these celebrations first begin? What are they celebrating? Are they celebrated country-wide? Why or why not? Widen the discussion by asking the children to think how they might perform a poem about a chosen festival. Then, as a class, choose one festival and write a performance poem together. Prepare to present it to other classes, perhaps at assembly. Encourage the children to use imaginative props and sound effects, if appropriate.

3 Using Ian Souter's poem, *Up the Stairs to Bed!*, as a model, the children could write their own **shape poems** based on the long, flowing Chinese dragon, using words that describe how it looks, moves, swirls and dances. The poem could be written down in a conventional form first and its eventual 'shape' sketched separately, so that the words fit and that it really looks like a dragon after completion.

Links to the pupil text

You might like to link this work with the work the children have been doing in the Pupil Book on performing the poems. How might they accompany a performance of their dragon shape poem? What sounds might it make as it swirls colourfully about?

Diwali by David Harmer

About the poem

This is a rhyming **performance poem**, designed to be said aloud by any combination of voices, from the solo performer to the whole class. The Hindu festival of Diwali, which takes place in late October to early November, celebrates the return of Rama and Sita to their kingdom after 14 years in exile. The goddess of wealth, Lakshmi, is welcomed into Hindu homes at this time to bring them prosperity. Part of the preparation for Lakshmi is the lighting of many lamps to greet her as she will not bless any home that remains in darkness.

Rhyme

The *light, night, sight* rhyme occurs three times and emphasises the shift in the rhythm at particular points in the poem. Other than that, the end rhymes are in pairs, so the scheme can be written as aabbaaccddaa.

Diwali

Bright blazing light,
burning up the night
drive the dark and cold away
make the nightime bright as day
bright blazing light
beautiful sight
from each window lamps will burn
Rama, Sita will return
to bring us wealth, bring us love
from the goddess high above
bright blazing light
this Diwali night

David Harmer

About the poet

David Harmer was born in 1952 and has been Headteacher of Rosedale Primary School for ten years. Many of his stories and poems for children and adults have appeared in a wide variety of collections, anthologies and magazines. David has run many workshops both for adults and in schools. He is currently undertaking an MA in Writing Studies.

Rhythm

Because the poem is written for performance, there are no verse breaks. The whole chunk of text is to be said in one go with no spaces to break it up. This adds pace and speed to the rhythm. The poem has deliberately been ended on the same two punchy lines that begin it, not just to give it unity but also to enable the piece to be performed as a round so that the beginning becomes the end, and so on. To vary the rhythm, sections of long lines have been contrasted with short ones and have also been reinforced with rhyme and **alliteration**. The line *bright blazing light* occurs three times, just after a section of longer rhythms, to bring the beat of the poem back into its swing and, at the same time, to reinforce the poem's meaning. The alliteration on the two opening words offers a stress that gives an almost drumming sound to the line, which thumps back in every time it is repeated.

Imagery

The image central to the poem is that of light driving out darkness. Images of fire *burning up the night* in *blazing light* have been used to reinforce this idea, and in the last two lines this imagery has been linked deliberately to Diwali itself. The poem also contains some general information about the celebration and its principal characters.

Suggested activities

1. The main purpose of this poem is to have it performed. The text is fairly simple and swings along well, so the real learning here is in how it is divided up between groups of voices and how they perform it. You could do it straight off the page, but some thoughtful variations can be built in. One section of the class, for example, could take up the *bright blazing light, burning up the night* **refrain** and keep it going alongside other voices narrating the main poem. Variations in the volume of each group would allow clarity, so that sometimes the refrain would be heard and at other times it would be whispered under the main body of the poem. The children could add percussion to parts of the poem to reinforce the beat (for example, a tambour playing under the *bright blazing light* lines) or the meaning (a cymbal smash after *goddess high above*). Another variation would be for the whole class to say the poem with vigour and expression down to the *beautiful sight* line and then build in a call and response section. One half narrates *from each window lamps will burn* and it is softly repeated by the other children. This can be done down to *goddess high above* then the whole class crash in with the final **couplet**, possibly repeating the last line for emphasis.

2. Performance poems rely on a simple text and many variations of voices, tone, mood, speed and volume in their delivery. It's those dynamics that give the performance poem its quality. A performance poem relies on a lot of repetition and two-, three-, four-part groupings. Sections can increase in volume, decrease, speed up, slow down, feature one voice (solo or group), two voices in unison but doing different parts, voice plus **chorus**, and so on – the variations are endless. It is important to begin with simple texts. A good start is the school's menu for the week's lunches or a simple recipe or a shopping list. It is the arrangement of the text and the way it is read that gives the poem its life, not the text.

3. Having used the texts suggested above, the children could assemble their own performance poems, for instance, pollution and litter make a good starting point. Make sure the poems do not get too complex, although simple choruses can help to swing it along well. This is an excellent group activity for the children to brainstorm around one large piece of paper. Once the final text has been assembled on another big piece of paper, they can stick it to the wall, stand round it and begin to annotate it to show how they intend to perform it. They then work up their performance. Page 23 shows a simple example of the way a poem could be assembled and scripted.

Links to the pupil text

You might like to link this with the work the children have done on writing descriptive **similes** in the Pupil Book. They might like to use their descriptions as further inspiration for decorating the large copy of the performance poem.

Scripting a poem

Chorus to be spoken by all twice:

"Litter litter everywhere
Thrown around without a care   } x 2
Rotten rotten litter! Rotten rotten litter!"

Now split into two groups, each takes a line in turn:

Group A	**Group B**
"Crisp packets	Sweet wrappers
Old bottles	Plastic bags
Newspapers	Chewing gum
Pop cans	and broken glass
Pop cans	and broken glass"

Repeat the chorus

Two groups:

Group B	**Group A**
"Old sofas	Bust-up bikes
Mattresses	Half a car
Burning tyres	Bits of wood
Shopping trolleys	Pram wheels
Shopping trolleys	Pram wheels"

Repeat the chorus

Then:

one voice
"What a mess!"

three voices
"What a sight!"

one voice
"Clean it up!"

six voices
"Shiny bright!"

Repeat this section, but this time with soft chanting underneath the main voices:

"What a mess, what a sight!"

Then:

one voice *building gradually to whole class:*

"What a mess, clean it up,"
"What a mess, clean it up, WHAT A MESS, CLEAN IT UP!"

Final chorus

Moonwatcher by Sue Cowling

About the poem

This poem has a regular rhythm pattern and a **regular rhyme** scheme. It is a poem playing with language, with an elusive quality to its language despite appearing straightforward in its meaning. The speaker in the poem is talking to someone about the moon and asking questions about it in six sets of **rhyming couplets**. Each **couplet** begins with a **portmanteau word**, where two words have been blended into one. The first part of the word is a verb and that is jammed onto questioning words: *what, why, how, where, who, when* respectively. This variation in everyday speech immediately holds the reader's attention. The couplets then narrate the poem from the moon appearing high in the sky to its going and the speaker wondering if it will return. All of this is done using delicate language that evokes a great sense of mystery. The questions are phrased oddly and the reader is unable to say who is asking questions of whom.

Moonwatcher

Speakwhat
Silver boat is that.

Saywhy
It sails lady-high.

Showhow
It is not there now.

Sharewhere
Is its thoroughfare.

Spellwho
Taught it what to do.

Tellwhen
It will come again.

Sue Cowling

About the poet

Sue Cowling lives near Birmingham and was a teacher. She wrote her first poem when she was nine and still prefers children's poems to grown-up ones. Most of hers are written sitting on the floor in a patch of sunshine or while out walking the dog. She likes words, the sea, chocolate and Christmas. She hates cruelty to animals and dusting.

Rhythm

Each couplet has the same syllable count. The first line has two syllables and the second line has five. The contrast between the short line and the longer line means that the question is punched out in two stressed words (with a 'tum-tum' rhythm) and then drawn into a slower pace. The two words, almost normal in themselves but made odder by being blended together, are asked first, as though the questioner is getting them out as quickly as possible, needing an answer. But then, as the beauty of the moon in the night sky entrances the speaker, the rhythm grows longer and the language becomes more expressive and far less straightforward, as evinced by *lady-high*. Whereas the first line seems purely functional, in the second line there is a sense of wonder and mystery. This effect is partly achieved through contrasting rhythms.

Rhyme

The rhyme is a very regular one of aa bb cc dd ee ff, although the first aa is more an **eye-rhyme** than one we hear – that is, it works as a rhyme on the page but doesn't quite rhyme when spoken. This is another example of **half-rhyme**. Another is the **assonance** between *sails* and *lady* in the fourth line of the poem. All the rhymes contribute strongly to the **cadence** and mood of the poem.

Suggested activities

1. Using Sue Cowling's portmanteau words, ask the children to write poems that answer those questions (or some of them), but in a totally different context. Give the children a frame that has the questions as a first line to a couplet for them to write the second. One suggested theme could be that of the school itself and some of the personalities in it. Again, it would be wise to abandon the limitations of rhyme, for example:

    Speakwhat
    rings loudly at ten to nine.

    Saywhy
    we all have to go to school!

    Showhow
    I can do my sums.

    Sharewhere
    I can play football.

    Spellwho
    is my favourite teacher.

    Tellwhen
    it is time to go home!

2. You might develop this by asking the children to swap poems with a partner so they can add a third or even a fourth line after each couplet, actually answering the question, for example:

    Speakwhat
    rings loudly at ten to nine.
    My alarm clock.
    I've overslept and now I'm late!

Flu by Tony Langham

About the poem

The underlying joke of this poem lies in the substitution of letters in words to give the idea of the speaker having flu. Its structure is interesting as no line has more than two words on it and many have only one. In the poem the letter *n* becomes a *d*, *t* becomes a *p*, and *v* and *p* become *b*. If it is said aloud, it really does sound like someone speaking with a very heavy cold. The poem ends with a **calligramic** device, showing the sneeze growing longer and louder.

Rhyme

The end of verse one rhymes with the end of verse two, as well as the word *do* on the third line of the second verse. All three rhyme with the final sneeze *achoooooooooooo!* These simple rhymes pull the poem together very effectively.

Rhythm

The very short lines give the poem a pacy rhythm, which is slowed down by the physical difficulty of actually saying some of the words. The reader cannot say them with any clarity because the substitute letters thicken the enunciation, as they would if the reader actually had flu.

Flu

Wed
yoube
gop
the flu

your dose
doesn't
do
what it's
subbosed
to do

achooooooOOOOOO!

Tony Langham

About the poet

Tony Langham currently teaches English to Pakistani and Bangladeshi children and writes poetry and stories for children of all ages. Tony is over 50 years old, and when he grows up he wants to be a painter of magical paintings which will tell people exactly how he feels about living on Planet Earth.

Suggested activities

1. The children will soon get the hang of the substitute letters device and enjoy writing their own poems that tell of their colds and coughs. You might give them a writing frame of using the sneeze as a **chorus** and putting two- or three-line verses inbetween. If the story of their poem is an attempt to get well, using the substitute letters rule, they could arrive at their last verse cured, only to sneeze again …

2. Ask the children to think up some other difficulties which might alter the spellings of words in a poem and its general layout. They could write a poem about having the hiccoughs, or a bad leg, or feeling dizzy. Remind them that writing a poem about being sleepy, or a poem spoken with a mouthful of sweets or an ice lolly would affect the layout of the lines and the way the words were spelled.

Bubble Trouble *by Ian Souter*

About the poem

This poem is written in **free verse**. This means it relies on the rhythms and **cadences** of natural speech. There is no regularity to its verse form as the first stanza is much longer than the second. Its comic effect lies in its rhymes. Again, these occur in an irregular manner and mainly rely on the repetition of key words. A poem as loose as this makes an interesting contrast to a poem such as the Sue Cowling poem, *Moonwatcher*, which, although not written in a conventional, metrically recognisable **scansion**, has a regular and repeated rhythmic pattern. Comparing the two poems shows some of the richness and diversity of contemporary poetry.

Bubble Trouble

You have some gum
And you blow a bubble.
Now if you were to blow another bubble
You could have a bubble-double,
And if you redouble the bubble
You could have a redoubled, bubble-double
Which could lead to trouble –
Especially if it BURST!

Just imagine:
Redoubled – trouble – double-bubble gum
Plastered all over your face.

Ian Souter

About the poet

Ian Souter is a teacher and a writer. His hobbies include most sports, computers, photography, music and reading. His favourite poets are Stanley Cook and Shel Silverstein. He lives in Hove, East Sussex with his wife and two children.

Rhyme

The *bubble/double/trouble* rhyme is central to the poem. The humour comes from the culmination of adding word upon word, rhyme upon rhyme, until the reader arrives at the visual joke at the end just after the tongue-twisting experience of the earlier lines.

Rhythm

The free verse allows the lines to expand and contract in length which affects how they are read. This, in turn, gives the poem its rhythm, which combines with the rhyme to give the poem its humour. By line six, for example, the reader is having to work through a long list of rhymes which gives the line a very lumpy rhythm. This makes the reader feel they really are chewing that gum! By the second line of the second verse, this device has made the line so difficult to read (and the physical difficulty of saying the words is, of course, part of its humour) that the poem is now almost at the level of a tongue twister.

Suggested activities

1. Using the poem as a model, the children could write a small free verse poem, of uneven verse lengths and irregular rhythms, about the perils of other foods. Food such as spaghetti, chewy meat, sticky jam buns, soup, spicy food and melting ice cream all pose threats to the person eating them. Suggest that, instead of rhyme, **alliteration** might help by lending a comic touch, for example, 'slurping slimy spaghetti' or 'chewing chunky chops'.

Says of the Week by John Foster

About the poem

This poem draws its humour from playing with words and making puns on the days of the week. The clever interplay of words and ideas, reinforced by word repetition and rhyme, make it a very witty poem.

About the poet

John Foster taught English for over 20 years and is now a full-time writer. He also edits poetry anthologies and writes information books and textbooks. His hobbies are swimming and skiing and he is a keen supporter of Carlisle United. He and his wife live in Oxfordshire.

Says of the Week

Money-day. Pay away day.
Choose day. Whose day?
Wedding's day. Thick or thin day.
Furs day. Wrap up warm day.
Fries day. Hot dog day.
Sat-a-day. Armchair day.
Sons day. Dads play.

John Foster

Rhyme

The rhymes, and this includes the repetition of the same word such as *day*, work horizontally through the lines and vertically down the lines. Line one has four rhymes in a row. Line two exactly balances two rhymes around the **caesura**. Line three **half-rhymes** *wedding* with *thin* and repeats the *day* rhyme. The following four lines then switch from picking up jokes through rhyming, to word associations. This culminates in the witty last line. The end rhymes of the poem all copy each other.

Rhythm

Although the chief features of this poem centre on word play and rhyme, John Foster does employ a sophisticated rhythmic device called the caesura. This is a pause or break in the middle of line suggested by the sense of the poem (reinforced here by full stops) which adds to the rhythm of the line and informs the reader on how to read it. The very definite stop in the middle of each line emphasises the call-and-response nature of the poem. It is almost as if each line was said by two different speakers, one asking a question, the other answering.

Puns

To the adult ear and eye, John Foster's jokes, though clever, are obvious enough. They must be pointed out carefully to the children, however, because the comedy of the poem relies on the accumulative effect of the puns as each one piles on the next. Added to this is the popular comedic effect of the puns growing ever wilder and more exaggerated. *Furs day. Wrap up warm day* is a tight pun with a logical feel. If for 'Thursday' the poet substitutes *Furs day*, then it is appropriate indeed to wrap up warm. The same logic underpins the last line, where Sunday becomes *Sons day* and their dads play with them. The jump from 'Tuesday' to *Choose day*, however, is a little harder to follow, although the response is logical. The same is true of 'Wednesday' somehow becoming *Weddings day*. These puns are likely to be received with an affectionate groan by adults which is why they are such fun!

Suggested activities

1. Taking each of the poet's lines as a starting point, the children could write a **list poem** of their own about that day. They can use either what really happens on that day to them both at school and at home, or they can follow the logic suggested by *Says of the Week*, for example:

   Son's day. Dads play.
   Down the park we take our ball.
   Dad goes in goal,
   I kick the ball, shoot and score.
   Every time a winner!

2. The class might find the concept of punning difficult, but they could try to write their own version of John Foster's poem by finding different ways to pun on the days of the week. Some examples might include 'Mum's day', 'Shoes day', 'Wendy's day', 'Thirsty day', 'Fly day', 'Splattered day' and 'Sung day'. Each pun would then need a response, either the rest of the line or several lines making a verse, following the logic suggested by the pun.

3. The children could generate similar poems based on other areas of their experiences. Puns could be based on, for example, the seasons, months of the year, meals on the school menu, names of pop groups, sweets, crisps and chocolate bars.

Links to the pupil text

You might like to tie these activities into the children's work on 'Knock-knock' jokes in the Pupil Book. Perhaps their poetry writing can be used as a basis for jokes which the children can perform in pairs for the class. Can the audience guess the final answer?

Full and Empty *by Clive Webster*

About the poem

This poem is made of six sets of **non-rhyming couplets** that all follow a very regular rhythmic pattern. The second line of each **couplet**, apart from the last, acts as a **repeating refrain** or **chorus**. The last line of the poem varies that refrain to give a dramatic and humorous conclusion to the poem's **narrative**. This poem also contains dialogue and a list of characters, introducing a giant who eats them all in the last two lines!

About the Poet

Clive Webster is a retired Head of English (in both Secondary and Middle schools). He worked as a teacher for five years in the Bahamas and still goes back there for holidays. As well as writing children's poetry his hobbies are amateur operatics, squash, snooker and golf.

Full and Empty

Henry said, "I could eat a house."
And he rubbed his empty tummy.

Shelley said, "I could eat a ship."
And she rubbed her empty tummy.

Martin said, "I could eat a mountain."
And he rubbed his empty tummy.

Wendy said, "I could eat the world."
And she rubbed her empty tummy.

The giant said, "I could eat you all."
And he rubbed his empty tummy.

And then he did it, just like that
And rubbed his full full tummy!

Clive Webster

Rhythm

Even though this is **free verse**, the rhythm of the poem is very regular. The first line of those couplets introducing characters by name begins with two syllables. The fifth couplet breaks this rule but the final couplet begins with two syllables as well. It also contains a **caesura** emphasised by a comma. The opening lines hardly vary, ranging from seven to nine syllables, and the **refrain** and concluding line are rhythmiclaly identical. The author uses **alliteration** to tighten up some of his lines. Each character's name begins with the same letter as the food they demand: *Henry* and *house*, *Shelley* and *ship*, *Martin* and *mountain* and *Wendy* and the *world*. Although this is not **metrical** verse, it is very tightly worked out. The reason is that the poem has a strong **narrative** which follows the tradition of the folk tale where a lot of repetition and refrain (perhaps called out by the listeners) leads to the conclusion of the story. Therefore, Clive Webster builds up a set of structured couplets in a repeated pattern, a requirement of the **genre**. The rhythm of the poem is integral to its traditional form and its meaning.

Narrative

As the story of the poem unfolds and each new character enters and begins to speak, their claims get larger and larger. The first character says he will eat a house, the second a ship, the third a mountain and the fourth the world. Then a giant enters who eats them all, thus presumably saving the planet! This measured escalation plus refrain is a stock device of the folk tale, as is the introduction of a giant who threatens all the characters. The rather dark humour of this poem is that the traditional ending is turned on its head and the giant wins. It is as though Jack never made it down the beanstalk! This puts a spin on the poem, demonstrating, as do many contemporary children's stories and poems, an anti-traditional twist in the plot. This usually leads to laughter – as it does in this case, as the giant, without much thought, merely devours the whining children.

Suggested activities

1. Taking the plot of a well-known tale, perhaps *Cinderella* or *Jack and the Beanstalk*, ask the children to write a poem telling the essential parts of the story using the Clive Webster poem as a model. The verses should be regular but could be more than two lines each, and there should be a repeated refrain that comes out of the story. The challenge is to write the poem, either as a class or as an individual activity, within no fewer than 12 and no more than 20 lines.

2. The title of the poem itself suggests a contrast. Using 12 couplets, or less, the children could write poems that explore other contrasts in which each couplet has a line dealing with each opposite, for example, a poem called 'Wet and Dry':

Martin said, "It's raining, I'm soaking."
Dad said, "Stay inside where its dry."
Shelley said, "I like swimming."
Dad said, "On the beach it's dry."
And so on.

This example takes a lot of ideas from the Clive Webster model, including a refrain, but that is only one suggestion. The contrasts could be in the verses and there might be no refrain at all.

3. Taking the idea of dialogue in a poem, the children could write a humorous poem that was almost all made up of dialogue. They could use conversations in the playground or from around school as their source. To keep the poem tight, they should use Clive Webster's idea of couplets plus a refrain, for example:

"_____" (line one)

"_____" (line two)

"And that's just what they said, that's just what they said." (suggested refrain)

Eyes Bigger Than... by Mike Johnson

About the poem

This is a nonsense poem that plays with the idea of taking a few simple rhyming lines and generally having fun by repeating them and reversing the order of some of the words.

Structure

The first line sets up the pair of rhyming problems of the poet who has eaten too much cake! The second line has a thumping rhythm, where four two-syllable words that either rhyme fully or **half-rhyme** (*gurgle* being the exception) use their qualities of **onomatopoeia** to sound like the poorly stomach. Line three, which rhymes with line one, tells the listener the source of the problem. Line four rhymes with its originator, line two. The third line is repeated, only there is a variation and the phrases are reversed but the rhythm and the rhyme are the same. Line six is the same as line two and rhymes with itself and line four. Line seven is the first line with the phrases reversed. The last line adds more onomatopoeia and is a repeat of line four. The **end-stop rhyming** scheme is abababab, however, this ignores the **internal rhymes** of *cake* and *mistake*, *quake* and *ache*, *rumble*, *mumble* and *rumble*, and half-rhymes *gurgle* and *grumble* that add so to the poem's vigour.

Eyes bigger than ...

belly ache, belly quake
rumble mumble gurgle grumble
chocolate cake, a big mistake
rumble mumble rumble
a big mistake, chocolate cake
rumble mumble gurgle grumble
belly quake, belly ache
rumble mumble rumble

Mike Johnson

About the poet

Mike Johnson has loved playing with words ever since he can remember and has been writing for children since 1989. He also works in schools – coming face to face with an audience is always exciting and challenging. Mike also teaches English and Creative Writing courses and is a volunteer at the local dogs' home.

Suggested activities

1. This is a poem to be performed with pace and expression, either by a group of children or the whole class. The refrain of *rumble mumble rumble* can be repeated or be used as a backing rhythm. (See pages 21–23 for further **performance poem** ideas.)

2. Children could write birthday party poems that end in upset stomachs, based on the theme of over-eating. The poem could start with the line 'chocolate cake, a big mistake' and continue from there, but not necessarily rhyming. A list of foods could produce a list of problems.

It's Not Fair by Christine Potter and Feet by Clive Webster

About the poems

Both poems are in **free verse**, although Clive Webster's is a lot tighter, thus offering a contrast to Christine Potter's longer, freer rhythms. Both poems are very funny, dealing as they do with themes that children will understand.

About the poets

Christine Potter read History and English at Leeds University. Chair of Pennine Ink Writer's Workshop, Burnley, she is a former compiling editor of *Pennine Ink*, the group's magazine. She is Associate Editor for Big Lamp Books, a community publishing project in Lancashire. She has had poems published in several anthologies.

For information about Clive Webster, see *Full and Empty*, page 30.

It's Not Fair

my mum said she'd smack me
if I did it again
so I did, and she didn't
so I did it again
and she did

it's not fair

Christine Potter

Feet

Feet.
They hold my legs up,
My feet.
Feet.
They keep my socks on,
My feet.
Feet.
They smell rotten,
My feet.

Clive Webster

Structure

Christine Potter gets her humour from the interplay of the phrases *so I did* and *I did it again*. She is dealing with a subject dear to every child's heart – the inconsistency of adult judgements and actions – and using one of the most common phrases of children. Clive Webster's poem is clearly influenced by Spike Milligan, and uses words like *sock*, and phrases such as *smell rotten* that are just about guaranteed to have children laughing. *Feet* is very regular in its pattern and structure. The *Feet* line, is followed by a longer line of four to five syllables followed by a **refrain**, before returning to *Feet*. It doesn't rhyme but repeats *Feet* six times (seven if you count the title).

Both poems make very good jokes.

Suggested activities

1. Using the title 'It's Not Fair', the children could list all the times it hasn't been fair for them. They could site verse one at school, verse two at home and verse three at the shops, on holiday or at Grandma's house. The **chorus** 'It's not fair, it's not fair, I'll tell you something, it's not fair' can be used to link the verses together. Remind the children that this is a **list poem** and should contain dialogue and real incidents. They should take quite a bit of time talking and drafting their work before the poems are made, as this is a rich source of real opinion and feeling for the children.

2. The poet Paul Cookson uses a similar method for getting classes of children to make **performance poems**. He teaches them a chorus: 'Nag nag nag, yap yap yap. Parents, teachers on your back'. The class then list all the lines they can referring to this and select the ones they want for their poem. They then divide the poem up and work on how to perform and present it.

3. Another idea is for the children to write the poem as the internal monologue of a child who, with the rest of the class, has been kept in because somebody did or said something and won't own up. This is never fair! Of course, another monologue could be the thoughts of the child who was responsible for the punishment in the first place.

4. The children could use Clive Webster's poem as a model, both in terms of structure and idea, to write a poem about different parts of the body. This could soon become fairly tasteless, but arms, legs, eyes, mouths, heads and ears seem fairly safe bets! Clive's joke is to transfer the function of the sock to the feet and the leg to the foot and this joke could be used by the children.

5. The structure of *Feet* is so clear and strong that it makes an excellent framework for any poem. The model needn't follow the exact syllabic count but the pattern is a good one, for example:

   1. Title: _____ (This could be any theme really. It would be interesting to contrast a serious subject with Clive Webster's poem, such as a season or a feeling, or love, hate, or friendship.)
   2. Title word
   3. Extended line (of four to six words to develop the theme)
   4. My _____ (plus title)

   And so on, continuing the pattern as presented by the poem.

Links to the pupil text

You might like to tie this work on body poems with the work the children have done on descriptions of parts of their bodies in the Pupil Book. How might they illustrate their poems?

The Wise Young Owl by Philip Burton

About the poem

This is a nonsense poem with echoes of *The Owl and the Pussycat* by Edward Lear. There are three verses of four lines each. This regularity of form is echoed by a **regular rhyming** scheme, strengthened by **half-rhyme** and a fairly regular rhythm.

About the poet

Philip Burton was born in Dunfermline, Scotland, and raised in Ramsgate, Kent. He retired as a primary school headteacher in 1995 and three years later he took up writing. His poem 'The Pocket Watch' was short-listed for the Kent and Sussex Open Poetry Competition. *The Wise Young Owl* is his first published poem for children.

Rhyme

The second and fourth line of each stanza rhyme. The scheme is abcb defe ghih. However, the first and third lines of the first and last stanza half-rhyme. This helps pull the poem together and contributes to its rhythmic feel. There is an example of **assonance** in the third line of stanza one with *bright* and *cried*, and in the second line of stanza three with *back* and *ratatat tat*.

The Wise Young Owl

Kylie reached up in the sky.
She broke off half a moon.
That's not so bright, the owl cried.
Be finished with it soon!

Kylie reached up in the sky,
and threaded the stars like beads.
She gave the necklace to the owl
who was utterly displeased.

The owl fixed the broken moon,
nailed back the stars with a ratatat tat.
What's down is down is down.
What's up is up is up. That's that.

Philip Burton

Rhythm

The poem has an easy, story-telling pace to it, especially in the first two verses. In the third verse, Philip Burton changes the rhythm slightly. Using **onomatopoeia**, he hardens the ending of line two and copies that firmness with a **caesura** in line four, the last line of the poem. The decisiveness of the young owl's wise action is emphasised rhythmically and the poem ends on two stressed beats: *That's that*. This emphasises the tone of the poem as, all the way through, the owl has disapproved of Kylie's actions. When things are put to rights by the owl and the night sky made whole again, the final *That's that* is far more than a cry of satisfaction – it is a firm warning from the wisdom of one creature concerning the foolishness of another. It means: 'Don't do that again. See what happens when you do? The trouble you cause?' The poet cleverly uses rhythm and rhyme to emphasise that meaning.

Imagery

The poem begins with a startling event and then introduces the character of the wise owl who is upset by Kylie's destructive actions. However hard Kylie tries to please, and in verse two Philip Burton uses a delightful **simile**, *she threaded the stars like beads*, the owl will have none of it. It repairs the damage, puts the universe back to rights and tells Kylie that is how it must stay. The only way a nonsense poem can work is if it has some strong link with real, everyday experience. If Kylie is the child, playing, experimenting, creating but causing upset and fuss, then surely the owl comes in with the adult response all the children in the class will recognise: 'Stop playing, put those things away and do as you're told. And that's that'. This message is translated by the poet into this magical, moonlit world where the stars become a necklace that can be hammered back into position and a bit of the moon can be broken off and then mended again. The poem has a charm and a vigour to it which keep it fresh and contemporary in feel, yet it works within a clear and well-established tradition.

Suggested activities

1. Nonsense poems have to have their own logic. In their own way they must 'make sense' and this can be hard for children to write. One way for them to begin is to continue the theme of Philip Burton's poem, though not the form, and to write about what Kylie did next to the sky. The owl's response would be important in the poem and it might be that in the end the owl is resigned to Kylie's actions and ignores them, or it accepts her presents and joins in.

2. Other devices for generating nonsense poems include encouraging the children to work with cut-up texts, like newspaper headlines, that are jumbled and have to be rearranged together in a different order. This exploits the natural sense the language makes, however odd the juxtapositions. Another idea is to play the game of consequences where the group begins by writing a line about the classroom and folding it over. This paper is passed round the group and the next person writes a line on the same thing. This procedure repeats all round the group until it is finished. No one sees what anyone else has written, until the whole thing is read out as one poem – in all its nonsensical glory.

3. Starting with the necklace of stars, the children could write a **list poem** of all the jewellery and beautiful gifts they would make from other things found in the sky. What would they make from the sun? Or from clouds, starlight, raindrops, icicles, snowflakes, hailstones and mist? The poem would be quite simple, starting with the line 'I made a necklace of stars'.

Links to the pupil text

You might like to link their work on nonsense poetry with *The Owl and the Pussycat*, the text of which is featured in the Pupil Book. Can the children find more poems by Edward Lear to add to a class display, or similar nonsense rhymes by other poets?

A Shaggy Dog Story by Marian Swinger

About the poem

This is a nonsense poem that is entitled after the kind of story nobody believes – it is not a poem that expects to be believed. Yet, it really is about a shaggy dog and as all nonsense poems do, has a tangible link with normality. The poem deals with impossible journeys and has an echo of *The Jumblies* by Edward Lear. There are three verses of four lines each with a strong regular rhythm and a **regular rhyming** scheme.

About the poet

Marian Swinger lives with her husband, a greyhound and a cat near the River Thames, about 50 kilometres from London. She is a full-time photographer and has three grown-up children and a seven-year-old grandson. She enjoys reading, painting, walking in the countryside.

Rhythm

The poem has an easily-paced, regular beat that carries the story along unobtrusively. It is emphasised by the repetition of the *shaggy dog* line at the beginning of each verse.

A Shaggy Dog Story

A shaggy dog went sailing
on the wild and windy sea.
He sailed off to Australia
and was back in time for tea.

The shaggy dog went flying
in a mini aeroplane.
He flew it round the moon
and then he flew it back again.

The shaggy dog went driving
in a tiny shiny car.
He drove across the Milky Way
and came back with a star.

Marian Swinger

Rhyme

There is a regular pattern to the poem's end rhymes where the second and fourth lines of each stanza rhyme. The scheme is abcb defe ghih. There is a good example of **assonance** in the first verse, line three, where the **half rhyme** depends upon vowels; *sailed* and *Australia*. There is also a lovely full rhyme in line two of the last verse which picks up the pace of the rhythm a little with *tiny shiny car*.

Imagery

The shaggy dog travels by three modes of transport: by boat, aeroplane and car. Of course, the humour of the poem lies in the way that the transport defies natural laws. The dog, despite *the wild and windy sea*, sails to Australia and is back by teatime! His aeroplane is capable of flying to the moon and back, and his car takes him into space to the Milky Way from where he returns with a star. Why he is doing all this and how a dog can manage all these vehicles remains, of course, unexplained and simply adds to the joke. Like all good nonsense poems, this poem has a strong internal logic that makes the shaggy dog's adventures quite believable.

Suggested activities

1. Marian Swinger has invented a wonderful character which is brave, intrepid and resourceful. There is no doubt that the shaggy dog could go anywhere, anyhow and do anything with great aplomb and success. The children could write poems that take the shaggy dog elsewhere and tell of his adventures. Again, the verse form of three stanzas of four lines is a good framework to follow but, unless it occurs naturally, rhyming is best avoided.

2. Using the storyline of one of the verses, the children could write a poem telling what happened on the dog's journey in that particular verse – they write a poem based upon one of Marian Swinger's verses.

3. Using the abcb rhyme scheme, the children could write a postcard poem from one of the places visited in the poem, in the role of the shaggy dog. They should stick to four lines when trying this. The activity concentrates on good rhyming that doesn't disturb the sense of the poem too much, although there is some room for interpretation here as it is nonsense verse.

Links to the pupil text

You might like to link this work with the children's writing of the shaggy dog's travels in the Pupil Book. Perhaps they could make a class anthology of his poems and stories, and mark where he travels on a 'fantasy map'.

PART TWO
Introduction

This poetry collection has been carefully selected to match the range required in the National Literacy Strategy (NLS) for each term of each year group in Key Stage 2. The selection for each term includes suggested teaching strategies and relevant questions to help teachers fulfil the NLS teaching objectives for each term at text, sentence and word levels. In each case we have indicated the specific part of each NLS reference that is fulfilled in the teaching strategies.

The poems have multiple uses and, although they fit the requirement of the teaching objectives for each term, they will also support teaching mixed age and mixed ability classes. The poems can be used in different year groups to fulfil teaching objectives but at the same time teachers can feel secure in the knowledge that the required objectives for each term are covered. Reference for use in different year groups is included whenever appropriate. In addition we have included some 'further interesting points to note', where appropriate, to draw out any further features of the poem that could be looked at.

As you become more familiar with the guidance, you will appreciate the wider opportunities for supporting and challenging children to appreciate and understand the many different and exciting forms of poetry. To do this, it is important that the children are led through the questions, to ensure full participation. For the purposes of fulfilling the requirements of the NLS, the teaching strategies are closely linked to the termly objectives. It is hoped, however, that the poems and suggested activities will inspire teachers and children to read and write poetry and to develop an enthusiasm for all forms of poetry.

Term 1

Wind *by Andrew Collett*

Range

Poems based on observation and the senses.

Introduction

Hide the title and read the poem through once. Ask the children if they know what the poem is about. Read it again, this time with the children joining in. As you read, stress the verbs clearly.

Text level work

- Y3T1TL6 to read aloud and recite poems, comparing different views of the same subject; to discuss choice of words and phrases that describe and create impact e.g. powerful and expressive verbs.
- Y3T1TL7 to distinguish between rhyming and non-rhyming poetry.
- Y3T1TL8 to express their views about a poem, identifying specific words and phrases to support their viewpoint.

Teaching strategies

- Point out the rhyming pattern of the poem (abcb defe ghih).
- Discuss the structure of the poem.
- Discuss the mood of the poem.
- Expect the children to justify their views.
- Point out the poet's personification of the 'wind'.
- Construct an extra verse with the children.

Questions to ask

- *Is this a rhyming or non-rhyming poem?*
- *What is the rhyming pattern?*
- *How does the poem make you feel?*
- *Do you like the poem? Why? Why not?*
- *What different verbs could you introduce for the sound of the wind?*
  What rhyming words could be used?
  How many syllables are there in each line? (The lines are five or six syllables.)

Sentence level work

- Y3T1SL3 the function of verbs in sentences.
- Y3T1SL4 to use verb tenses with increasing accuracy in speaking and writing.
- Y3T1SL5 to use the term 'verb' appropriately.

Teaching strategies

- Point out the different verbs used in the poem.
- Experiment with changing the verbs.
- Note the verb tense used in the poem (present).
- Create new lines of poetry with the children using different verbs. Compare the different verbs.
- Illustrate the verbs using **pictograms**.

Questions to ask

- *Which verbs do you think are the most effective?*
- *How effective do you think the new verbs are?*
- *What is the verb tense? Why do you think the poem is in this tense?*
- *Which verbs work best?*
- *How can you write and illustrate the verbs so that they give a picture of movement?*

Word level work

- Y3T1WL16 to understand the purpose and organisation of the thesaurus, and to make use of it to find **synonyms**.
- Y3T1WL18 to use the term 'synonym'.

Teaching strategies

- Check the children's understanding of the term 'synonym' (different words which have the same or similar meaning).

- Ask the children to find the synonyms in the poem (*pulls* and *tugs*, and *charges* and *dives*).

- Using a thesaurus, compile a class glossary of synonyms for use in constructing a new poem.

Questions to ask

- *What is a synonym? Can you provide some examples?*

- *Can you find any synonyms in this poem? Can you suggest some more synonyms for some of the words in the poem?*

- *What synonyms can you find to replace the verbs in the poem, for example, replace* stare *with 'glare'?*

Differentiation: links to other terms

Year 3, Term 3: Y3T3TL15 to write poetry that uses sound to create effects, e.g. **onomatopoeia**, **alliteration**.

- Talk about the words in the poem that use sound to create an effect, e.g. *rattles*, *creaks*, *roars* and discuss the words that the children found to describe the sound of the wind. Encourage the children to use as many of these words as they can in their own onomatopoeic poems. Encourage them to think of a title, such as 'Wind', that lends itself to an onomatopoeic poem. Other possibilities might be 'Rain', 'The River', 'Thunder' or 'Factory'.

- Discuss the poet's use of alliteration, for example, *whispers on windows*. Ask the children to think of a few new alliterative phrases and then work them into their poem.

> Blow, wind! Come, wrack! At least we'll die with harness on our back.
>
> William Shakespeare
> (Macbeth, v.v)

Term 1

Song *by Mary Green*

Range

Poems based on observations and the senses.

Introduction

Read the poem through once and then discuss the title and theme. Ask the children to try to invent new and different titles. If possible, compare different poems previously read on the same theme, perhaps asking the children to carry out some research in the book corner. Ask the children to describe the seasons using the poet's words. Then read the poem two or three times, encouraging the class to join in.

Text level work

- Y3T1TL6 to discuss choice of words and phrases that describe and create impact, e.g. adjectives, powerful and expressive verbs, e.g. 'stare' instead of 'look'.
- Y3T1TL12 to collect suitable words and phrases, in order to write poems.

Teaching strategies

- Discuss the layout and pattern of rhyme in the poem (aa a bb b cc c dd d).
- Identify all the rhyming words (there are many).
- Note the use of powerful and expressive adjectives and verbs, for example, *cloud gazey, summer yearning*.
- Collect phrases from the poem containing verbs and adjectives and discuss their impact.
- Construct a poem substituting some different adjectives and verbs but maintaining the meaning of *Song*. Use a flip chart or sentence wall to produce a class chart to explain the process of constructing a poem, based closely on this poem. You could include points such as brainstorming, initial shaping, drafting, revising, proof-reading and presentation.
- Invent different poems for a class collection based on the theme of seasons, perhaps making a class anthology for display.

Questions to ask

- *What is the structure of the rhyme pattern in the poem?*
- *How many rhyming words can you find?*
- *Which are your favourite verbs/adjectives?*
- *What is unusual about some of the descriptive phrases?*
- *Can you think of some different adjectives or verbs that would fit in the poem without changing the meaning?*

Sentence level work

- Y3T1SL2 to take account of punctuation.
- Y3T1SL3 to collect and classify examples of verbs from reading and own knowledge.
- Y3T1SL4 to use verb tenses with increasing accuracy in speaking and writing.
- Y3T1SL5 to use the term 'verb' appropriately.

Teaching strategies

- Note the function of individual verbs and adjectives in the poem.

Questions to ask

- *What is the purpose of the verbs? What is the purpose of the adjectives?*

Sentence level work *continued*

- Collect some verbs for the children to use in their own poem.

- Discuss the significance of the word order (for instance, that the adjective comes after the noun).

- Ask the children to note the absence of punctuation and add some punctuation of their own.

- *What verb tense has the poet used? Why has she used the present tense? What do you think spring, summer and autumn do?*

- *Can punctuation be added? How does this change the poem? Why do you think the poet decided not to use punctuation?*

Word level work

◆ Y3T1WL13 to collect new words from reading and work in other subjects and create ways of categorising and logging them, e.g. personal dictionaries, glossaries.

Teaching strategies

- Make a class list of the words in the poem ending in '-ing' (*ringing, ting-a-linging, winging, swinging, singing, turning, yearning, twirling, curling* and *swirling*).

- Categorise them as verbs which have spellings that do not alter when '-ing' is added.

- Add some more verbs with spellings that don't change when '-ing' is added to the class list.

Questions to ask

- *What type of words end in '-ing'? (They are verbs.)*

- *Can you think of any more?*

- *Ask the children to look in other poetry books for more '-ing' verbs.*

Differentiation: Links to other terms

Year 2, Term 1: Y2T1WL4 to investigate and classify words with the same sound but different spelling.

- Collect the different spelling patterns in words with the same sounds, for example, y<u>ea</u>rning, tw<u>ir</u>ling, c<u>ur</u>ling.

Further interesting points to note

- Help the children to discriminate syllables in multi-syllabic words using words from reading.

- Remind them what syllables are. Choose some words from the poem, asking the children to clap the syllables as you read them.

- Encourage the children to spell two-syllable words containing double consonants. Pick out the two-syllable words containing double consonants – *ruffle, bluffle, snuffle, duffle*. Can the children work out the rule, that it is a double consonant after a short vowel? Ask them to learn the words using the 'look, say, cover, write, check' strategy. Can they think of any other words with double consonants like this, such as 'battle', 'ripple', 'bubble'? They could also think of some more made-up words, such as 'bluffle'.

> As time requireth, a man of marvellous mirth and pastimes, and sometime of as sad gravity, as who say: a man for all seasons.
>
> Robert Whittington

What is Sharp? *by John Foster*

Range

Poems based on observations and the senses.

Introduction

Read the poem aloud to the children. Discuss the title and content of the poem, identifying the title as a question which the content of the poem answers.

Text level work

- Y3T1TL6 to read aloud and recite poems.
- Y3T1TL7 to distinguish between rhyming and non-rhyming poetry.
- Y3T1TL12 to collect suitable words and phrases, in order to write poems.

Teaching strategies

- Read the poem with the children using rising intonation for each answer to the title question. Stress the rhyming words (*pin, sting, grin, chin, nail* and *tail*).
- Ask the children to perform the poem repeating the title question before each verse.
- Extend the poem by adding further written answers to the question and making a class list.
- Use the framework of the poem to construct a question and answer poem for another title, for example, 'What is hot?', demonstrating to the children how to do this as a shared writing activity.

Questions to ask

- *What is the form of the poem? Is this a rhyming poem? What is the rhyme pattern?* (It is abcb dbeb fghg.)
- *How does reading the poem in this way change the effect of the poem?*
- *How does the length of each line help the poem?* (It keeps it short and sharp, tying in with the title.) *How many syllables are there in each line?* (Three to five syllables.) *Are there any unusual answers to the question, What is sharp? For example, 'How can a witch's grin be sharp?'*

Sentence level work

- Y3T1SL1 to use the awareness of grammar to decipher new or unfamiliar words, e.g. to predict from the text.

Teaching strategies

- Ask the children to identify any unfamiliar vocabulary and to make a list.
- Experiment, using different adjectives to describe the nouns used in the poem, for example, 'a silvery axe', 'a hissing snake'.

Questions to ask

- *How can you work out the meaning of these words? What clues are there on each line?*
- *What new words could you use to describe some of the words in this poem? Do different adjectives make it easier to understand the meaning of the poem?*

Word level work

- Y3T1WL17 to generate **synonyms** for high-frequency words.
- Y3T1WL18 to use the term 'synonym'.

Teaching strategies

- Explore the use of different titles of the same meaning using the poem as a starting point before moving on to other examples, such as 'What is big?', 'What is large?'

- Explore the use of opposites, for example, 'What is hot?', 'What is cold?'

Questions to ask

- *Could the title be changed? What is another word for* sharp? *How many words with the same meaning can you find for* sharp?

- *How many opposite titles can you list?* (You might like to provide some guide words to keep the activity focused.)

Differentiation: Links to other terms

Year 3, Term 2: Y3T2TL4 to choose and prepare poems for performance, identifying appropriate expression, tone, volume and use of voices and other sounds.

Year 3, Term 2: Y3T2TL11 to write new or extended verses for performance based on models of 'performance' and oral poetry read.

- Ask the children to use the question and answer form of this poem as a model for their writing, or use the work they have done in the class. Once they have written the poem, they could work in pairs to perform it, one child posing the question, the other answering it. Before the performance they should work on the tone, volume and expression of their voices.

- Individual children might also write a 'question and answer' poem as an independent writing activity.

Year 3, Term 3: Y3T3TL15 to write poetry that uses distinctive rhythms.

- Discuss how the poet uses the form and rhythm of the poem to reflect its subject. Ask the children to think of subjects for poems and say how they think the form of the poem could be used to mirror the title, for example, 'What is clumsy?' could have long, meandering lines, 'What is jerky?' would have lines with a lot of punctuation to break them up. The children could then use these ideas to write their own poems.

'Tis a sharp remedy, but a sure one for all ills.

Reportedly said by
Sir Walter Ralegh
as he felt the axe's edge before his execution

Term 1

Nature Shapes *by Sue Cowling*

Range

Poems based on observations and the senses.

Introduction

Read the poem through once to the class. Discuss the title. Do the children think it is a good title? Why or why not?

Text level work

- Y3T1TL6 to read aloud and recite poems.
- Y3T1TL12 to collect suitable words and phrases in order to write poems.

Teaching strategies

- Read the poem to the children again but ask them to join in with the last word of each verse. Encourage them to use appropriate emphasis.
- Count the syllables in each line, clapping the pattern of the **rhyming couplets**.
- Inform the children about rhyming couplets.
- Collect the **similes**, e.g. *as tough as a telephone cord*.
- Invent new similes to use in rhyming couplets. Give the children some starting points, such as 'as thorny as _____, as bendy as _____, as scorched as _____'. Then collect several examples for each one. When you have a dozen examples, ask the children to brainstorm suitable rhyming words and, finally, to put the couplets together.

Questions to ask

- *Do you like the poet's choice of words? Why? What techniques does the poet use to create emphasis?*
- *What is the rhyming pattern?* (It is ab cb de fe.)
- *What is a simile?* (When something is compared to something else.) *Which simile do you like best in the poem, and why?*

Sentence level work

- Y3T1SL2 to take account of punctuation.

Teaching strategies

- Discuss how the punctuation is used to create effect, for example, the use of the dash and exclamation mark.
- Ask the children to add punctuation to the rhyming couplets they composed as part of their text level work.

Questions to ask

- *What is the punctuation used in the poem? When would you use an exclamation mark? When would you use a dash?*

Word level work

- Y3T1WL13 to collect new words from reading and create ways of categorising and logging them, e.g. personal dictionaries, glossaries.

Teaching Strategies

- Make a list of expressive terms which would be appropriate to replace the words at the end of each line. Make sure the children provide some lively word suggestions.

- Identify new and interesting vocabulary, for example, *networks, tendrils*. Check that the children understand the meaning of the words by writing their own definition, ready for a class discussion. The children could then create their own poetry work using new words they've found.

Questions to ask

- *What different words would you choose for the last word in each verse?*

- *Which words are new to you? What do you think they mean?*

Differentiation: links to other terms

Year 4, Term 2: Y4T2TL5 to understand the use of figurative language in poetry and prose.

- Extend the children's understanding of similes by explaining that expressions such as *like a railway track* is a way of using figurative language to create an image. Encourage the children to find other uses of figurative language in the poem and to try to explain why the poet has used those particular expressions.

Year 4, Term 3: Y4T3SL2 to identify the common punctuation marks, including dashes, hyphens and exclamation marks, and to respond to them appropriately when reading.

- Remind the children why dashes and exclamation marks are used in this poem. Ask them to consider how this makes them read the poem. Encourage them to reread it as if it had no punctuation. Can they hear the difference?

Further interesting points to note

- The children could write a poem based on the structure of *Nature Shapes*, using a rhyming dictionary to compose their rhyming couplets.

Man is Nature's sole mistake!

W.S. Gilbert (Princess Ida)

Term 1

Weather Band by Celia Warren

Range

Poems based on observations and the senses.

Introduction

Discuss the title with the children. Ask them to predict what the poem is going to be about. What is a *Weather Band*? Now read the poem, emphasising the sound words, for example, *whistling, thumping, rapping*.

Text level work

- Y3T1TL6 to read aloud and recite poems, comparing different views of the same subject; to discuss choice of words and phrases that describe and create impact, e.g. powerful and expressive verbs.
- Y3T1TL7 to distinguish between rhyming and non-rhyming poetry and comment on the impact of the layout.

Teaching strategies

- Read the poem again to the children. Discuss and compare it with other weather poems they know, for example, *Wind* by Andrew Collett.

- Reread the poem, this time stressing the sound of the verbs. Compare the use of verbs in *Weather Band* and *Wind* (verbs are used in the present tense in *Wind* and in the present participle in *Weather Band*).

- Compare the layout and shape of the poems.

- Compare the rhyme of both poems.

- Discuss the use of **metaphors** in *Weather Band*. For example, the wind is described as a *piccolo*. (The main metaphor of the poem uses musical instruments.)

- Compare the poem with *Nature Shapes* by Sue Cowling, which uses **similes**.

Questions to ask

- *In Andrew Collett's poem* Wind, *the wind is described as a person. How is the wind described in this poem?*

- *Can you substitute different words, or verbs, that create sound effects?*

- *How many lines are there in each verse of both poems?* (Two lines in *Weather Band* and four in *Wind*.) *Which poem uses couplets?* (*Weather Band*.)

- *Which words rhyme in* Weather Band? (*Piccolo* and *window* are **near rhymes**, and *door* and *floor*.) *Are the poems slow or fast moving?* (*Weather Band* is the quick-moving poem.)

- *Can the wind really be a* piccolo? *Can the rain really be a* banjo? *What other words could you use to describe the wind or the rain?*

- *What is the difference between a simile and a metaphor?*

Sentence level work

◆ Y3T1SL3 the function of verbs in sentences.

Teaching strategies

- Note the poet's use of verbs at the beginning of each second line.

- Raise the children's awareness about the use of the present participle '-ing'. With the children, construct lines of verse beginning with different verbs, such as 'banging'.

Questions to ask

- *Do we usually start sentences in prose with a verb? Can you think of any examples?*

- *What does thunder do? (Thunder is ... thumping.) What tense does the poet use? How does each verb end in this form of the present tense? What different verbs could be used instead?*

Word level work

◆ Y3T1WL8 how the spelling of verbs alters when '-ing' is added.

Teaching strategies

- Identify the words ending with '-ing' (*whistling, thumping, rapping* and *rattling*). Write them on a flip chart for the children to see.

- Ask the children to work out the root words for each one ('whistle', 'thump', 'rap' and 'rattle').

- Make a chart, identifying the rules that have changed each word.

Root word	Add '-ing'	Rule
whistle rattle	whistling rattling	drop the 'e'
thump	thumping	no change
rap	rapping	double the 'p'

Questions to ask

- *Which words end in '-ing'?*

- *What are the root words of each of these? How has each changed when '-ing' is added?*

- *Which words follow the same rule? (They are 'whistle' and 'rattle'.)*

Further interesting points to note

■ Children might like to write poetry that uses sound to create effects, for example, **onomatopoeia**. Discuss some suitable topics that lend themselves well to using onomatopoeia. For example, traffic, natural forces (rivers, earthquakes) and computer games.

■ The strongest element of this poem is that it uses onomatopoeia to create sound effects. **Assonance** is also used to add to the effect. More able children could be challenged to use onomatopoeia and assonance in their writing.

There is really no such thing as bad weather, only different kinds of good weather.

John Ruskin
as quoted by Lord Avebury

Term 1

Fish by Ruth Underhill and Crescent Moon by Sue Cowling

Introduction

Ask the children what they think these poems look like. Discuss the shape of *Fish* and how the size and shape of the words have been changed, and how the second line curves in *Crescent Moon* to contribute to the poem.

Range

Shape poems.

Text level work

- Y3T1TL7 to comment on the impact of the layout.
- Y3T1TL13 to invent **calligrams** and a range of **shape poems**.

Teaching strategies

- Read each poem, pointing to each word.

- In *Fish*, discuss the position of each line of the poem, for example, *Flip Flap Fin*. (The words are situated in the position of the fish's fin.)

- Again focusing on *Fish*, discuss the last line of the poem, *Bite The End*, which is written to make the tail.

- Construct a fish-shape poem using different, but appropriate, words, for example, 'Slippery, Silvery Fish'.

- Compare *Fish* with *Crescent Moon*. Discuss how, although both poems use features of word shape to extend the poem, *Crescent Moon* uses the feature in one line only.

- Check the definition of calligram. Ask the children to think of suitable topics for which they invent calligrams.

Questions to ask

- *Which line should be read first?* (The top line in each case.)

- *Which words in each line should be read first? Does the word position contribute to the poem?*

  Could the poem be read in a different way? Why not?

- *Is the end of the poem effective? Why?*

- *Could you substitute different words in the fish poem? Could you construct a different ending?*

- *How are* Fish *and* Crescent Moon *the same? How are they different? Which poem do you prefer? Why?*

- *Do you know about calligrams? Do the letters form the shape of this poem? Is this poem a calligram?*

Sentence level work

- Y3T1SL2 to take account of grammar and punctuation.

Teaching strategies

- Compare the two shape poems. Read each one.

- Discuss the use of punctuation and capitalisation, or lack of it.

- Inform the children that poets often break the conventions of sentence grammar, but that it is done with a purpose.

Questions to ask

- *Which poem contains a sentence?* (*Crescent Moon*.)

- *Which poem contains punctuation?* (*Crescent Moon*.)

- *How do the two poets use capitals?* (In *Fish*, the initial letter of each word is capitalised, but in *Crescent Moon* it is the first word of each line only.)

Word level work

♦ Y3T1WL6 to use independent spelling strategies, including using visual skills, e.g. recognising common letter strings.

Teaching strategies

- Identify the consonant clusters 'spl', 'fl', 'sh', 'gg'.

- Collect words with similar letter clusters.

- Demonstrate how to remember the spelling of *Crescent*, that it has 'scent' inside. Then discuss 'sent' as opposed to 'scent'. Relate this spelling pattern to other 'sc' words, such as 'crescendo'.

Questions to ask

- *Can you remember how to spell* Crescent*? How many words can you find that contain 'scent'? What about words that contain 'sent'?*

Further interesting points to note

■ Refer back to the use of **alliteration** in *Fish*. Which words in *Fish* are **onomatopoeic**? (*Splish, Splash, Flip, Flap, Wiggly*). Can you think of some more? Which words are alliterative? (*Splish Splash, Flip Flap Fin, Wiggly Worm*.) Why do the children think the poet has used alliteration? (It creates the impression of the sounds of the fish in the water.) Do they think it makes the poem more exciting and alive?

■ Draw the children's attention to *Wiggly*. Ask them to spell other two-syllable words containing double consonants you give them, such as 'bubble', 'kettle', 'common'.

■ The more able children will enjoy making two-syllable words with double consonants to describe fish or worms. The words can be real, like 'fiddly' and 'tiddly', or invented.

> For spirits when they please
> Can either sex assume, or both; so soft
> And uncompounded is their essence pure ...
> in what shape they choose.
> Dilated or condensed, bright or obscure,
> Can execute their aery purposes.
>
> John Milton
> (Paradise Lost, Book 1)

Up the Stairs to Bed!
by Ian Souter

Range: Shape poems.

Introduction

Introduce the poem by asking the children what the shape of the poem looks like. What type of poem is it? Read the poem at a steady beat whilst marching to depict climbing up stairs.

Text level work

- Y3T1TL6 to read aloud and recite poems, comparing different views of the same subject.
- Y3T1TL7 to comment on the impact of the layout.

Teaching strategies

- Read the poem again with the children but change the pace so you are reading at a slower pace. Then try reading it at a faster pace.

- Discuss the shape of the poem and compare it with *Fish* by Ruth Underhill. Identify the differences between the two.

- Discuss the length of the lines in *Up the Stairs to Bed!* and count the number of words in each.

- Identify the rhyming words in *Up the Stairs to Bed!* and list them.

- Construct different **shape poems** using the same theme of going to bed.

Questions to ask

- *How does the poem make you feel? What is the effect of reading the poem at a slower pace? How do you think the poem should be read? Why?*

- *What are the different shapes? Which shape describes the object of the poem?* (The fish in *Fish*.) *Which shape describes the idea of the poem?* (The stairs in *Up the Stairs to Bed!*)

- *All lines in the poem have only one word except for one line of three words in the middle. What effect is the poet trying to achieve? Has he managed it?*

- *What is the rhyming pattern?* (*Steep* and *asleep* are the two rhyming words.)

Sentence level work

- Y3T1SL2 to take account of punctuation.

Teaching strategies

- Discuss the only punctuation used in the poem (the exclamation mark).

- Discuss the reasons why the poet may have decided not to use any more punctuation (for example, to give the feeling of continually walking up the stairs).

Questions to ask

- *What effect does the exclamation mark have when used at the end of the poem?*

- *Why do you think no other punctuation is used? How does it make us read the poem?*

Tir'd Nature's sweet restorer, balmy sleep!
He, like the world, his ready visit pays
Where fortune smiles; the wretched he forsakes.

Edward Young
(The Complaint: Night Thoughts)

Animal Sneezes by Roger Stevens

Term 1

Range: Shape poems.

Introduction

Cover the poem and read the title. Ask the children to try to predict the different animals that might be included in the poem before reading it. Look at the poem with the children and compare the different sizes of print used.

Text level work

- Y3T1TL6 to read aloud and recite poems.
- Y3T1TL7 to comment on the impact of the layout.
- Y3T1TL13 to invent a range of **shape poems**.

Teaching strategies

- Select individual children to provide the sneezes as you read the poem.
- Discuss reading with expression and intonation.
- Ask the children to perform the poems both solo and in **chorus**.
- Construct different shape poems to picture different sneezes.

Questions to ask

- *Which animal will sneeze quietly? Which will sneeze loudly?*
- *How does the frog sneeze? How does the dog sneeze? What different intonation can be used for these animals? How does the layout make us read the poem? How might a snake sneeze?*
- *What different ways could the poem be read?*

Sentence level work

- Y3T1SL2 to take account of punctuation.
- Y3T1SL9 to notice and investigate a range of other devices for presenting texts.

Teaching strategies

- Identify the use of the exclamation mark.
- Identify the different sizes of print and the way the frog's sneeze is written. Experiment with other fonts and handwritten forms in the children's own work.
- Make a comic strip which illustrates different animal sneezes.

Questions to ask

- *Why is the exclamation mark used? Does it change how you read the poem?*
- *How might you illustrate different sneezes?*

There was an old man of Slough,
Who danced at the end of a bough;
But they said, "If you sneeze,
You might damage the tree,
You imprudent old person of Slough."

Edward Lear
(One Hundred Nonsense Pictures and Rhymes)

Term 2

Caribbean by Anita Marie Sackett

Range

Oral and performance poetry from different cultures.

Introduction

Point out to the children that the first letter of every line forms the title. Inform them that this poem is called an **acrostic**, then ask the children to define an acrostic poem in their own words. Begin to compile a list of definitions of different types of poems for a class chart of, for example, rhyming poems, non-rhyming poems, **shape poems**, and so on. (You might like to refer to the glossary at the back.) Now read the poem aloud in a lively rap style.

Text level work

- Y3T2TL4 to choose and prepare poems for performance, identifying appropriate expression, tone, volume and use of voices and other sounds.
- Y3T2TL11 to write new or extended verses for performance based on models of 'performance' and oral poetry read, e.g. rhythms, repetition.

Teaching strategies

- Read the poem with the children so they gain a picture of what the poem is about. In twos, encourage them to read the pairs of rhyming lines of poetry alternately, so one child reads two rhyming lines, then the second child reads the next two, and so on.

- Identify the changing pattern of the rhyme, for example, the first two lines don't rhyme, the next four rhyme in pairs and the last three rhyme.

- Read the poem using body music or percussion accompaniment, perhaps using a tambour, rhythm sticks or shakers.

- Encourage the children to dance to the rap rhythm of the poem as you click your fingers or the children stamp their feet (this could be a part of a dance and movement lesson). Discuss why there is a strong rhythm to the poem (to reflect the Caribbean carnival).

- Ask the children to construct a poem for their own area, or any region studied for geography. Model the composition of a class poem in shared writing with the whole class.

Questions to ask

- *What does the poem describe? Where is the poem set? What do you notice about the rhyme pattern?*

- *How does the rhyme pattern change?*

- *How does the rhythm help the poem? Is the pace of the poem fast or slow? Does it add to the Caribbean feel of the poem?*

- *How could the poem be performed to a dance movement? What different movements could be used?*

- *List useful describing words for a different area and culture. Which words would be most effective in a poem?*

The strong sea-daisies feast on the sun.
Algernon Charles Swinburne
(The Triumph of Time)

Sentence level work

- Y3T2SL2 the function of adjectives within sentences.
- Y3T2SL6 to note where commas occur in reading and to discuss their functions in helping the reader.

Teaching strategies

- Emphasise the adjectives when reading the poem.

- Encourage the children to provide different adjectives that are still appropriate to the poem, and to invent new ones similar to *sunsplash beat*. Write a class list of all the adjectives, both real and invented.

- Look at the line *Anancy, trickster spider man*. Explore and discuss the impact of the comma before looking at the commas on the other lines.

- Write a list of adjectives to describe an object, for example, 'the wood is smooth, shiny, oblong, short and hard'. Discuss the use of commas in lists. Then return to the commas at the end of the lines. Compare the poem with the list the children have written and discuss the effect.

Questions to ask

- *What do the adjectives do?*

- *Are any of the adjectives invented? Can you think of some alternative adjectives which are real words? Can you invent some new adjectives?*

- *Why are commas used? What is the purpose of the comma in this poem?*

- *In what way is the poem similar to a list? What tells you that? Does it change how you read the words?*

Word level work

- Y3T2WL17 to continue the collection of new words from reading and work in other subjects, and make use of them in reading and writing.

Teaching strategies

- Identify new or unfamiliar words, for example, *Anancy*, *poinsettia*, *breadfruit*.

- Ask the children to use dictionaries to find the meanings of each unfamiliar word. Ask them why they think *Anancy* is not in the dictionary (because it is a proper noun, or a name).

Questions to ask

- *Are any of the words in the poem unfamiliar?*

- *What do you think they might mean? How could you find out? Can you guess what or who* Anancy *is? Now you all know what a mango is, why do you think the poet describes the moon as a mango? What else could you describe as a mango?*

Differentiation: Links to other terms

Year 4, Term 2: Y4T2TL7 to identify different patterns of rhyme and verse in poetry, e.g. choruses, rhyming couplets, alternate line rhymes and to read these aloud effectively.

- Remind the children of the changing pattern of rhyme they found in Caribbean. Discuss the fact that it is not a regular rhyming scheme. Ask the children to write the end of line rhyming scheme using letters (abccddeee).

Year 4, Term 3: Y4T3TL5 to clap out and count the syllables in each line of regular poetry.

- Ask the children to clap out the rhythm of the poem in the same way as you did when snapping your fingers during the text level work. Encourage them think about how the words break into syllables when they do this, for example, car/ni/val. Point out that this is a good strategy for learning unfamiliar spellings.

Term 2

Chinese New Year in China Town
by Andrew Collett

Range

Oral and performance poetry from different cultures.

Introduction

Before reading the poem, discuss the title and ask the children to predict the content of the poem. Where is the poem set? What is the time of year? What would they expect to find in the poem? Read the poem through once using a lively, bouncy rhythm.

Text level work

- Y3T2TL4 to choose and prepare poems for performance, identifying appropriate expression, tone, volume and use of voices and other sounds.
- Y3T2TL11 to write new or extended verses for performance based on models of 'performance' and oral poetry read, e.g. rhythms, repetition.

Teaching strategies

- Compare the two poems *Caribbean* and *Chinese New Year in China Town*. Read both poems with the children.

- Compare the pace of both poems.

- Now focus on *Chinese New Year in China Town* and note the repetition of the first two lines at the end of the poem.

- Note the first line of each new verse which, apart from the first verse, contain a short, simple line of two words.

- Construct short, two-word lines to introduce possible new verses, for example, 'crackers snap'.

- Ask the children to prepare a performance of the poem themselves in small groups.

Questions to ask

- *How is the rhythm different between the poems? What is the rhyming pattern in both? How are the rhyming patterns different for each poem?* (*Caribbean* is abccddeee and *Chinese New Year in China Town* is abcb defe ghih jbkb.)

- *Do the poems have a similar pace, or are they different? Why do you think that is?* (*Chinese New Year in China Town* is the faster-paced poem, denoting the excitement, crowds and flurry of a new year.)

- *Why do you think the poet repeats the first lines?* (One reason might be that the repetition offers closure to the poem, making it circular and reflecting the circular dance of the dragon.)

- *What do you notice about the start of each verse?*

- *Can you list different ideas for a new verse of poetry?*

Sentence level work

- Y3T2SL6 to note where commas occur in reading and to discuss their functions in helping the reader.
- Y3T2SL7 to use the term 'comma' appropriately in relation to reading.

Teaching strategies

- Encourage the children to identify the use of commas where they allow a pause in reading.

Questions to ask

- *What is the purpose of the comma in verses one, two and three?*
- *For what other purpose is a comma often*

Further interesting points to note

- If necessary, remind the children what verbs are by drawing their attention to their use at the beginning of each verse (*shoot, dance, twist*). Ask the children, 'What are the lanterns doing?' 'What are the faces doing?' Point out that the writer also uses the '-ing' form of a verb (the present participle). Do the children think this is because the poet wants to explain what the lanterns or faces have done or are doing?

> Will you, won't you, will you, won't you, will you join the dance?
>
> Lewis Carroll
> (Alice's Adventures in Wonderland)

Term 2

Diwali *by David Harmer*

Range

Oral and performance poetry from different cultures.

Introduction

Ask the children to identify the country of origin for the poem and discuss their previous knowledge and understanding of the festival of Diwali. Can they predict what might be contained in the poem? Ask the children if they have any questions which have been raised by the poem or the illustration.

Text level work

- Y3T2TL4 to choose and prepare poems for performance, identifying appropriate expression, tone, volume and use of voices and other sounds.
- Y3T2TL5 rehearse and improve performance, taking note of punctuation and meaning.

Teaching strategies

- Read the poem aloud, maintaining a brisk pace and without pausing. Now read again more slowly.

- Compare *Diwali* with *Chinese New Year in China Town*. Compare known and researched information about the different festivals.

- Note the repetition *bright blazing light* and the effect it has on the poem.

- Identify the main image of the poem (that of light driving out darkness).

- Encourage individuals, or small groups, to recite these repetitions. Then model a different way of performing the poem with the whole class as a shared reading activity (see Suggested activities on page 22).

- Ask the children to invent their own methods for performance. Encourage them to rehearse and improve their performance.

Questions to ask

- *What do you think about the poem being read so quickly? Does it suit the content? What is the effect of keeping a quick pace? Which is the most effective – reading slowly or quickly?*

- *How are the poems different? How are they the same?* (They are set in different countries and are written in different styles. They are both about festivals, however, and the welcoming of something new – whether the new year or the arrival of light driving out darkness.)

- *What is the bright blazing light? Why does the poet repeat the line? How many different ways could the poem be read?*

- *What pictures, or images, do you see in the poem? Which is the most important picture? What do you think the poet wants you to see?*

- *Experiment in groups of four. Find two different ways of performing the poem.*

- *How differently can you use your voice? Consider the difference volume, tone and expression will make to your performance.*

Sentence level work

- Y3T2SL6 to note where commas occur in reading and to discuss their functions in helping the reader.
- Y3T2SL7 to use the term 'comma' appropriately in relation to reading.

Teaching strategies

- Note the use of one comma to embed a clause in the eighth line and the use of a comma in the first line.

Questions to ask

- *Does the poet use the comma extensively? Why not? What is the purpose of the commas he has used? Are the commas used for different purposes?*

Word level work

- Y3T2WL17 to continue the collection of new words from reading and make use of them in reading and writing.

Teaching strategies

- Focus on the **alliteration** in the poem and collect the words using the same initial letters, for example, *bright, blazing, burning, beautiful*.
- Ask the children to use these collected words in a different way in their own poems, for example:
  Her beautiful, blazing hair
  Shone brightly as she danced …
  Some children may find it easier to write nonsense poetry.
- Ask the children to collect some more alliterative words from reading other poems, and to use them in their own poems.

Questions to ask

- *How effective are the alliterations used in this poem? What do they add to it? Do they make it easier or more difficult to read?*
- *Can you construct a new line of poetry about something different using the words we have just collected?*

Further interesting points to note

- Help the children to identify and read different patterns of rhyme and verse in poetry, for example, **choruses**, **rhyming couplets** and alternate line rhymes, by asking them to write the rhyming pattern using letters (aabbaaccddaa). Discuss the fact that the *light* and *sight*, *light* and *night* rhymes are repeated on the shorter lines, which emphasises the change in rhythm.

> I'll have them fly to India for gold,
> Ransack the ocean for orient pearl.
>
> Christopher Marlowe
> (Doctor Faustus)

Term 3

Moonwatcher *by Sue Cowling*

Range

Poetry that plays with language.

Introduction

Read the poem through once to the children. Ask them what they think the poem is about. Who is watching the moon? Ask the children to recall times when they watched the moon and compare what they saw with *Crescent Moon*, also by Sue Cowling (Term 1).

Text level work

- Y3T3TL7 to select, prepare, read aloud and recite by heart poetry that plays with language.

Teaching strategies

- Read the poem again with the children. As you read, emphasise the first line of each **couplet** so the children can easily spot the rhymes and combined initial words.

- Ensure that the children understand that the poet has combined two words to make a **portmanteau** word.

- Explain the difference between statements and questions by separating out the portmanteau words, such as 'Speak. What? Say. Why?'

- Ask the children to read the poem aloud in pairs or groups. Ask them to stress the rhyming words as they read. Inform them that this is a poem with **rhyming couplets**.

- Ask the children to write a poem by using the first words of each couplet and writing their own second line. Provide a frame to help them. (See Suggested activities on page 25.)

- Ask the children to learn their poems by heart, before performing them. Some children could 'share' a poem, learning only a line or two if they find this difficult. Discuss ways in which the children could learn their poems, for example, learning by repetition, by recording the poem on tape, by learning key phrases.

Questions to ask

- *What do you notice about the first line of each couplet?*

- *What special device has the poet used for the first lines?*

- *Which word in the portmanteau word is the question? Which word is a statement or command using a verb?*

- *What do you notice about the rhyming pattern?* (The pattern is aa bb cc dd ee ff.) *How do the first and second lines of each rhyming couplet differ?* (In length.) *How many syllables are there in each line?* (There are two in the first word and five in the second.)

- *What is the mood of the poem? How is the moon described? Can you think of different words to use in each second line?*

Word level work

- Y3T3WL12 to continue the collection of new words from reading and work in other subjects.

Teaching strategies

- Collect some new words and word combinations based only on the portmanteau words in *Moonwatcher*, for example, 'speakwhere'.

- Now ask the children to invent some different examples, for example, 'whisperhow'. You could write a list of appropriate words on a flip chart and suggest the children combine them in different ways. They could then use the words for a shared writing activity in preparation for an attempt at independent writing (for the more able children).

Questions to ask

- *Which new words do you like best? Why?*

Differentiation: Links to other terms

Year 4, Term 3: Y4T3SL3 to understand how the grammar of a sentence alters when the sentence type is altered, when, e.g. a statement is made into a question.

- Explore how to turn a command, such as *Speakwhat* into a polite request. Remind the children of the difference between questions and statements (or commands) as you suggest the example might be, 'Could you please tell me … ?' and 'Tell me … '

Year 5, Term 1: Y5T1TL8 to investigate and collect different examples of word play, relating form to meaning.

- Remind the children of the work done on portmanteau words and ask them how this form relates to the meaning of the poem (it enhances the sense of mystery). Then ask them to consider what other themes might be suitable (for example, a poem about the mysteries of the sea). Ask the children to think of other types of word play and to consider how they could be used for different themes. You might initiate a shared writing activity in which the children use their own ideas to prepare a poem, for example, words with letters missing in a poem about magic; a poem with mis-spelled words as a deliberate code for a spy; a poem written in reverse about going back in time.

Further interesting points to note

- The poem uses interesting **metaphors** for the moon. Investigate writing metaphors from original ideas by asking the children to look at phrases such as *Silver boat* and *sails lady-high* and to substitute their own metaphors. Or give the children unfinished phrases, into which they write their own metaphors, for example:

  The sun is …
  The moon sails …
  The stars in the sky …

- Compare this with the use of metaphor in Sue Cowling's *Crescent Moon* (Term 1) to make sure the children are clear about the meaning of the term.

It is the moon, I ken her horn,
That's blinkin' in the lift sae hie;
She shines sae bright to wyle us hame,
But, by my sooth! she'll wait a wee.

Robert Burns
(Willie Brewed a Peck o' Maut)

Term 3

Flu *by Tony Langham*

Range

Poetry that plays with language.

Introduction

Read the poem through with the children. Ask them about the type of poem it is. Do they like it? Does it make them laugh? Why? What is the shape of the poem?

Text level work

◆ Y3T3TL6 to compare forms or types of humour, e.g. by exploring, collecting and categorising form or type of humour, e.g. word play, joke poems.

Teaching strategies

- Read the poem again. Ensure the children notice the substitution of letters.

- Discuss the overall shape and form of the poem, and also the line lengths. Discuss the shape of the last line with the change in type size.

- Compare this poem with other humorous poems and/or **shape poems**, for example, *Bubble Trouble* by Ian Souter.

- Model composing a poem about colds or coughs using the substitution technique (as a shared writing activity).

- Encourage the children to use their library to collect other forms of joke poems and word plays. Compile a list of the different types of poem that they find.

Questions to ask

- *What trick has the poet used to make the poem sound as though it is spoken by a person suffering from flu?*

- *What do you notice about each line? How long are they? What size are they? What do you notice about the last line?*

- *What is a **calligram**?* (A poem in which the shape of the letters fits the poem's meaning.) *How can you illustrate words in different ways using calligrams?*

- *What letters does the poet change? Would you change different letters? Can you write some new words changing letters in the same way?*

Sentence level work

◆ Y3T3SL4 to use speech marks and other dialogue punctuation appropriately in writing and to use the conventions which mark boundaries between spoken words and the rest of the sentence.

Teaching strategies

- Discuss how spoken words and dialect can often be written how they are said and not how they are spelled.

- Ask the children to think of some ways in which words are said in their regional dialect (or choose another well-known dialect, if necessary).

- When the children have chosen some words, model a few lines of a poem. Remind the children to use speech marks and punctuation.

Questions to ask

- *How do we usually know when a word is written in dialect?* (It is in speech marks.)

- *Where do we use speech marks? What other punctuation do we need?*

Word level work

- Y3T3WL5 to identify mis-spelled words.

Teaching strategies

- Look at words that the poet has mis-spelled. Extend this to a discussion of any words the children commonly mis-spelled, for example, 'could of' rather than 'could have' and 'gonna' instead of 'going to'. Make a class list with both the incorrect and the correct spellings.

- Make the link that spelling is often driven by speech by drawing the children's attention to those examples on the list that demonstrate it, for example, 'gonna'. Relate this to the spellings in *Flu* as an extreme example.

Questions to ask

- *Are there words you know you often spell wrongly? Can you remember how to spell them correctly? Can anyone else provide the correct spelling?*

- *Do you think the poem would be as effective if it were correctly spelled? Why not?*

Further interesting points to note

- As well as using the mis-spelling of words device, the poet has also used apostrophes for contraction. Help the children to distinguish between the apostrophe being used for contraction and for possession.

- Ask them to find the words that have apostrophes in them in the poem, and to tell you whether they are for possession or contraction (in the poem they are used for contraction). Ask them to think why they think contractions have been used rather than the long form (to enhance the idea that it is someone who is speaking, rather than a poem that is written).

> I have caught
> An everlasting cold;
> I have lost my voice
> Most irrecoverably.
>
> John Webster
> (The White Devil)

Term 3

Bubble Trouble *by Ian Souter*

Range

Poetry that plays with language.

Introduction

Discuss the title with the children. Can they predict the content of the poem? Does the title sound familiar? Has the poet 'borrowed' his idea for a title? From where might he have borrowed it? (The witches chant, 'Double trouble' in Shakespeare's *Macbeth*.) Ask the children to compare *Bubble Trouble* with the **rhyming couplets** 'Double trouble':

Double, double toil and trouble
Fire burn, and cauldron bubble.

Read the poem *Bubble Trouble* once. What type of poem is it?

Text level work

- Y3T3TL6 to compare forms or types of humour, e.g. by exploring, collecting and categorising form or type of humour, e.g. word play.
- Y3T3TL7 to select, prepare, read aloud and recite by heart poetry that plays with language or entertains; to recognise rhyme, **alliteration** and other patterns of sound that create effects.
- Y3T3TL15 to write poetry that uses sound to create effects, e.g. **onomatopoeia**, alliteration, distinctive rhythms.

Teaching strategies

- Read the poem with the children. Compare it with other tongue twisters they know, such as *Peter Piper*, *She Sells Sea Shells* and *Betty Bought a Bit of Butter*.

- Discuss the rhythm and rhyme and ensure the children understand that this poem is an example of **free verse**.

- Discuss the humour of the poem.

- Model the construction of a poem in free verse using the example of a different sort of food, jelly being a good subject. Select a new title like 'Wibble Wobble' and, as a whole class shared writing activity, use a frame to write it:

  You have ...
  And you ...
  Now if ...
  You could have ...
  Which could ...
  Especially if ...
  Just imagine ...

Questions to ask

- *How is this poem the same or different compared with other tongue twisters that you know?*
  How does the poet develop the poem?

- *Does the poem rhyme? Which is the most difficult line to read? (You could have a redoubled, bubble-double.) Why?*
  Is there a pattern to the rhyme?

- *Which do you think is the funniest line? Why? Which is your favourite line? Why?*

- *Which different words would you substitute if you were eating jelly? What about this example:*

  You have some jelly
  And you wibble a wobble.
  Now if you wibble a wobble
  You could have a wobble double,
  And if you redouble the wobble
  You could have a redoubled wibble wobble
  Which could lead to trouble –
  Especially if it **wobbles**!
  Just imagine!

Sentence level work

◆ Y3T3SL2 distinguishing the 3rd person form of pronoun 'you'.

Teaching strategies

- Make sure the children can identify the use of the pronoun 'you' throughout the poem.

- Practise changing the pronoun 'you' to 'I' or 'we' and investigate what happens.

Questions to ask

- *Who do you think the poet is talking to? How do you know?*

- *What is the effect of changing the pronoun to the first person? Does the poem work as well using a different pronoun?*

Word level work

◆ Y3T3WL6 to use independent spelling strategies, including building from other words with similar patterns and meanings, spelling by analogy with other known words, e.g. light.

Teaching strategies

- Compare *Bubble Trouble* with the poem *Eyes Bigger Than …* by Mike Johnson.

- Collect all the words from *Bubble Trouble* that sound the same but are spelled differently (*bubble, double, redouble* and *trouble*). Explore which spelling is the more common.

- Collect some different words with the double consonant pattern, such as 'wibble', 'wobble', 'tipple', 'topple'.

Questions to ask

- *Which words sound the same, or rhyme? Which words sound the same and are spelled the same? Which are spelled differently? Which spelling occurs most often?*

- *Which of these words sound the same but are spelled differently?*

Further interesting points to note

- Secure the children's knowledge of exclamation marks in reading by emphasising the word *BURST!* when reading the poem. Discuss what purpose the capital letters and exclamation mark have. (They give extra emphasis to the word because something that bursts makes a loud noise and can give you a shock.)

- Reinforce the children's recognition of the common punctuation marks, including dashes and hyphens, and make sure they respond to them appropriately when reading.

- Discuss why the poet uses a dash at the end of line seven (to ensure the reader pauses briefly while reading it, and to emphasise the suddenness of the bubble bursting). Discuss also the use of the dashes in line ten (to show the increasing build-up of the bubble gum). Ask the children to read the poem aloud, taking account of how the dashes affect the reading of it.

> Mun, a had na' been the-erre
> abune two hours
> when – *bang* – went saxpence!!!
>
> Punch (vol 54)

Term 3

Says of the Week *by John Foster*

Range: Poetry that plays with language.

Introduction

Read the title and the poem with the children. What do they think the poem is about? What is funny and special about this poem? How has the poet got his idea for the title?

Text level work

- Y3T3TL6 to compare forms or types of humour, e.g. by exploring, collecting and categorising form or type of humour, e.g. word play, joke poems, word games, absurdities, nonsense verse.

Teaching strategies

- Write the days of the week on a chart and write the poet's days of the week alongside.

- Compare the words chosen by the poet with those of the days of the week.

- Discuss the form of the poem – that it is a word followed by a full stop followed by a definition.

- Define a pun, providing an example from the poem. (Puns are words or phrases that exploit innuendo or ambiguity in meaning, and they are usually humorous in intent.) Display the definition for the children all to see.

- Reinforce the idea of punning by asking the children to spot the puns used by the poet.

- Model the construction of alternative puns that could be used in the same poem, for example, 'Mum's day'.

- Ask the children to perform the poem in pairs so one child reads the word and the other reads the definition.

Questions to ask

- *What has the poet tried to achieve in changing the spelling of the words for the days of the week?*

- *Which words do you like best? Why? Which do you think are funniest?*

- *What do you notice about each line of verse? Why is the full stop used? Which are the nonsense words?*

- *What is a pun?*

- *How many different puns are used by the poet? What are they?*

- *There are lots of different puns that could be used for the days of the week. How many can you think of?*

  Can you write your own 'days of the week' poem using the different puns?

Sentence level work

- Y3T3SL7 to become aware how sentences can be joined in more complex ways through using a widening range of conjunctions in addition to 'and' and 'then'.

Teaching strategies

- To identify the use of the full stop in the middle and end of each line.

- Ask the children to think of conjunctions that could be used instead of the full stops in the middle of the lines. For example, 'Choose day <u>but</u> whose day?' or 'Furs day, <u>so</u> wrap up warm day'.

Questions to ask

- *What do you think the poet's purpose is when using the full stop?*

- *What effect does using the conjunctions have? How does it change how you read it?*

Word level work

- Y3T3WL5 to identify mis-spelled words.
- Y3T3WL12 to continue the collection of new words from reading and work in other subjects, and making use of them in reading and writing.

Teaching strategies

- Compare mis-spelled words with the correct spellings for the days of the week.

- Discuss the author's clever use of vocabulary and new meanings for familiar words.

- Invent some new, different words for days of the week (see Suggested activites, page 29).

Questions to ask

- *Which new words do you like best? Why? Which ones are the most like the correct spellings?*

- *Which of the definitions do you think provide the most meaning? Which definitions are most difficult to understand? Why?*

Differentiation: Links to other terms

Year 6, Term 2: Y6T2TL4 to investigate humorous verse: how poets play with meaning; nonsense words and how meaning can be made of them; where the appeal lies.

- More able children could discuss in depth why the puns are funny. They may point out the accumulated effect of the puns and note how the more exaggerated puns, for example, *Choose day*, are funnier. They may be able to evaluate the appeal of puns and give examples of where puns are used regularly (e.g. advertising, newspaper headlines, songs).

> What! keep a week away? seven days and nights?
> Eight score eight hours? and lovers' absent hours,
> More tedious than the dial eight score time?
> O, weary reckoning!
>
> William Shakespeare
> (Othello, III.iv)

Full and Empty *by Clive Webster*

Term 3

Range: Humorous poetry.

Introduction

Read the title and the poem with the children. What is the poem about? What type of poem is it? Does the poem make them laugh? Why? What is so absurd about this poem? Where did the poet get the idea for this poem?

Text level work

- TY3T3TL6 to compare forms or types of humour, e.g. by exploring, collecting and categorising form or type of humour, e.g. absurdities, cautionary tales, nonsense verse.

Teaching strategies

- Read the poem with the children again. Ask them to **chorus** the second line of each verse as you do.

- If necessary, inform the children that the poem contains **non-rhyming couplets**.

- Compare this with the **rhyming couplets** in *Moonwatcher* by Sue Cowling. Inform the children that this is a **narrative** poem.

- Identify the **alliteration** used for each character's name and the objects they could eat.

- Have the children heard the expression 'I could eat a horse'? Can they work out the meaning of the expression? Do they think it might have sparked off the idea for this poem? The poet develops the idea by thinking of more and more absurd things that the characters want to eat.

- Discuss the unexpected ending of the poem.

- In shared writing, model extending the verses or substituting different characters and different objects, for example, 'Robert said, "I could eat a ranch".' In another lesson you could model constructing a poem using dialogue and a different theme, such as 'I could swim a mile'.

Questions to ask

- *What is the pattern and form of this poem? Is the repetition of the second line effective? Why?*

- *Does the poem tell a story? Do you think the story is real or imaginary?*

- *What are the characters' names? What are the objects that each character says they can eat?*

- *How do you think the poet came up with the idea for the poem? How does he develop it?*

- *Were you surprised at the ending? Was is it funny? Why? (Because it is unexpected.) Do you think the characters deserved to be eaten because they were greedy?*

- *What different expressions could you substitute in the poem?*

Sentence level work

◆ **Y3T3SL4** to use speech marks and other dialogue punctuation appropriately in writing and to use the conventions which mark boundaries between spoken words and the rest of the sentence.

Teaching strategies

- Identify the use of speech marks and commas to mark dialogue. List the different uses of the comma on a chart. Explore the use of speech marks and commas in other texts with which the children are familiar.

- Write a copy of the poem on a flip chart, but leave out the punctuation. Ask the children to mark in the correct punctuation. Remind the children of the chart you have prepared, if necessary.

Questions to ask

- *What comes after* said*? Why do you think there are commas after* said*?*

- *Can you add the necessary punctuation?*

Word level work

◆ **Y3T3WL13** to collect **synonyms** which will be useful in writing dialogue, e.g. 'shouted', 'cried', 'yelled', 'squealed', exploring the effects on meaning, e.g. through substituting these synonyms in sentences.

Teaching strategies

- Over time and from other reading materials, collect alternative words, or synonyms, for *said*, for example, 'cried', 'shouted', 'squealed' and 'yelled'. Ask the children to substitute these synonyms in the poem and write it out again. You might suggest that the words could get louder in meaning as the poem progresses to reflect the increasing exaggeration, for example, 'Henry whispered', 'Shelley called' and 'Martin shouted'. Alternatively, more able children could try to think of alliterative synonyms that go with the names, for example, 'Henry hinted', 'Shelley shouted' and 'Martin murmured'.

- Ensure the children know and understand the term 'synonym'. Provide the information, if necessary, that it is a word that means the same as another word.

Questions to ask

- *How does changing the word* said *affect the poem? Does it change how you read it?*

- *Which synonyms are most effective? Why? What is a synonym?*

Differentiation: Links to other terms

Year 4, Term 3: Y4T3TL15 to produce polished poetry through revision, e.g. deleting words, adding words, changing words, reorganising words and lines, experimenting with figurative language.

■ The children could write their own poems based on this poem. They could do one or all of the following, depending on their prior knowledge of poetry. They could produce lines of what people said (remind the children to think of alternatives for *said*) or take the idea of writing a narrative poem with a surprising twist at the end. They could use the idea of exaggeration and take something else that people commonly exaggerate, such as 'I'm freezing' or 'You've asked me that hundreds of times'. Each child should produce several drafts before copying out their final version.

> Hunger is the best sauce in the world.
>
> Miguel de Cervantes
> (Don Quixote, Ch 5)

Term 3

Eyes Bigger Than...
by Mike Johnson

Range

Humorous poetry.

Introduction

Read the title with the children and ask them what they think it means. Check their knowledge and understanding of the expression 'eyes bigger than your belly'. Ask the children to provide examples of times when their 'eyes were bigger than ...' and how they felt.

Text level work

- Y3T3TL7 to select, prepare, read aloud and recite by heart poetry that plays with language or entertains; to recognise rhyme, **alliteration** and other patterns of sound that create effects.
- Y3T3TL15 to write poetry that uses sound to create effects, e.g. **onomatopoeia**, alliteration, distinctive rhythms.

Teaching strategies

- Read the poem through with the class.

- Ask the children to join in on the alternate lines (the 2nd, 4th, 6th and 8th).

- Read the poem again, this time asking the children to **chorus** the other lines (the 1st, 3rd, 5th and 7th).

- Ask the children to rearrange the word order of the lines, for example, *rumble mumble gurgle grumble* becomes 'grumble rumble mumble gurgle'.

- Define onomatopoeia (the use of words that sound like their meaning).

- Identify the sound words (onomatopoeia) and make a list on a flip chart.

- Invent more sound words that could be used to describe an upset stomach.

- Perform the poem in different ways. Children can experiment in guided or independent groups. Encourage the children to learn the poem by heart before reciting it.

- Compose a different poem using a similar technique. Model one example in shared writing with the whole class, perhaps drinking too much cola.

Questions to ask

- *Which lines are repeated? What do the lines say?*
  What is the overall pattern of the poem?

- *How does the poet play with the order of the words?*
  How is the word order changed? Can you change the order of the words to make a different version? Which lines do you think are most effective?

- *Which words sound like their meaning? What is onomatopoeia?*

- *In what different ways could the poem be read?* (By individuals, pairs, the whole group.) *What other ideas could you use as a basis to invent a similar poem?*

- *What onomatopoeic words could we use?* (Suggest 'slurp' or 'gurgle'.)

Sentence level work

- Y3T3SL7 to become aware of the use of commas in marking grammatical boundaries within sentences.

Teaching strategies

- Identify the commas used in the poem.

- Discuss the purpose and use of the commas and possible alternative ways to punctuate the poem.

Questions to ask

- *Why do you think the poet has used commas? Would you use commas in the same way?*

- *Would you add commas anywhere else in the poem? Why?*

Word level work

- Y3T3WL6 to use independent spelling strategies, including using visual skills, e.g. recognising common letter strings and checking critical features, spelling by analogy with other known words.

Teaching strategies

- Identify the words in the poem that have similar letter patterns (*mumble, rumble, grumble*). Ask the children to collect more words with similar patterns, for example, 'stumble', 'fumble', 'humble'.

- Identify words that rhyme but have different letter strings (*ache, quake, cake, mistake*).

Questions to ask

- *Which is the most common letter pattern used? Why has the poet used this pattern?*

- *Which words rhyme but use letter combinations that are not similar?*

Some physiologists will have it that the stomach is a mill; – others, that it is a fermenting vat; – others again that it is a stew-pan; – but in my view of the matter, it is neither a mill, a fermenting vat, nor a stew-pan – but a *stomach*, gentlemen, a ***stomach***.

William Hunter
(A Treatise on Diet)

Term 3

It's Not Fair *by Christine Potter*

Range

Humorous poetry.

Introduction

Discuss the title with the children. Can they predict the content of the poem? Ask 'What do you think is not fair?' Now read the poem. Note the repetition of the title in the last line. Discuss how often the children use the expression, 'It's not fair'.

Text level work

- Y3T3TL6 to compare forms or types of humour, e.g. by exploring, collecting and categorising form or type of humour, e.g. word play, joke poems, word games, absurdities, cautionary tales, nonsense verse, **calligrams**.

Teaching strategies

- Check the children's understanding of the poem. Can they recognise that the poet is speaking as though she were a child?

- Rewrite the poem together, as a class activity, as though the poet was the mother:
  I said I'd smack him/her
  If he/she did it again
  he/she did and I didn't smack him/her
  he/she did it again
  I smacked him/her
  it is fair

- Can the children grasp the change in perspective?
  Discuss the different points of view between the mother and child.

- Discuss the inconsistency of the mother's response.

- Ensure the children understand that the poem is **free verse**.

- Construct different poems entitled 'it's not fair when … '.

Questions to ask

- *Is it really not fair to be told off for doing something you shouldn't do?*
  Do you agree with the poet? Have you ever felt like this?
  Who is the poet pretending to be?
  Do you think a child should be smacked?
  Is the poem funny? Why or why not?

- *Which version of the poem do you think is most effective? Why? Do you think there is more humour when it is the mother who is telling the tale?*

- *How does changing the person who 'writes' the poem affect it?*

- *How is the mother's response inconsistent? (She doesn't carry out her initial threat.)*

- *Does the poem rhyme? What type of poem do we call this?*

- *List all the times you can remember when you've thought, 'It's not fair'.*

Sentence level work

- Y3T3SL2 to identify pronouns and understand their functions in sentences through distinguishing personal pronouns.
- Y3T3SL7 to become aware of the use of commas in marking grammatical boundaries within sentences.

Teaching strategies

- Use *It's Not Fair*, and the altered version from the mother's point of view, to discuss the use of the first person pronoun 'I'. Make sure the children understand the terms 'first person' and 'third person'.

- Discuss the different gender pronouns 'he' and 'she'.

- Note the punctuation (the apostrophe for contraction and a comma), how it is used and why.

Questions to ask

- *How does changing the poem from the third person to the first person affect the poem? What does first person mean? What does third person mean?*

- *Why has the poet used the comma? Why has she used the apostrophe?*

Word level work

- Y3T3WL17 to practise correct formation of basic joins from the use of the four basic handwriting joins from Year 2.

Teaching strategies

- Ask the children to copy the poem, in best handwriting, using diagonal joins for 'ai', 'it', 'id'.

- Note the consistency in size of letters and spacing between words.

- Ask the children to illustrate the poems and then to make a class book with them.

Differentiation: Links to other terms

Year 4, Term 1: Y4T1TL7 to compare and contrast poems on similar themes, particularly their form and language, discussing personal responses and preferences.

- Ask the children to find other poems about a child's relationship with his or her parents, for instance, *Mary, Mary, Quite Contrary*, or *There Was a Little Girl Who Had a Little Curl*. More able children may be able to point out the similarities and differences in form and language, and then to write their own poems on a similar theme.

> *He never wants anything but what's right and fair; only when you come to settle what's right and fair, it's everything that he wants and nothing that you want. And that's his idea of a compromise. Give me the Brown compromise when I'm on his side.*
>
> Thomas Hughes
> (Tom Brown's Schooldays)

Term 3

Feet *by Clive Webster*

Range

Humorous poetry.

Introduction

Read the title and the poem with the children. Emphasise the word *feet* as you read. Ask the children 'What do feet do?' and have a discussion on both sensible and silly ideas.

Text level work

- Y3T3TL6 to compare forms or types of humour, e.g. by exploring, collecting and categorising form or type of humour, e.g. joke poems.

Teaching strategies

- Read the poem again with the children. Ask them to **chorus** the 1st, 3rd, 4th, 6th, 7th and 9th lines.

- Rewrite the poem using dialect for *my* throughout the poem ('me legs', 'me socks'). Make sure the children understand the difference between standard English and dialect, and that dialect is not wrong.

- Rewrite the poem using a question and answer format, for example:

  What holds up your legs?
  My feet.
  What keeps your socks on?
  My feet.

  Ask the children to read it in pairs.

- Use a different title, such as 'My hands'. Give the children a frame to follow so they rewrite the poem for different body parts, following the same pattern. You might like to provide trigger words to keep the activity under control! You might suggest ears, eyes, nose, toes:

  Hands
  They keep my arms in place.
  They keep my gloves on.
  Hands
  They get really dirty.

- Compare the type of humour used in the poem with that of previously studied poems, for example, *It's Not Fair* and *Full and Empty*.

- Draw up a chart to categorise the types of humour.

- Ask the children to find different examples of humour.

Questions to ask

- *What is the pattern of repetition?* (The words are all *feet*.)

- *Which version is standard English? Which is dialect? What is dialect? Which version do you prefer? Why?*

- *Are all these poems funny for the same reason?*

- *Can you think of other ways a poem can be humorous?*

Sentence level work

- Y3T3SL7 to become aware of the use of commas in marking grammatical boundaries within sentences.

Teaching strategies

- Identify the commas and full stops in the poem.
- Identify the one-word sentences. Point them out to the children.
- Identify the two-word sentences and differentiate them from the one-word sentences.
- Identify the longer sentences which use a comma and full stop.

Questions to ask

- *When does the poet use commas and full stops? Why does the poet use commas?*

Word level work

- Y3T3WL6 to use independent spelling strategies, including recognising common letter patterns, such as 'ee'.

Teaching strategies

- Identify the 'ee' pattern in *feet*.
- Collect other words with the same pattern, for example, 'sweet'.
- Collect words that sound the same but are spelled differently, such as 'meet' and 'meat'.

Differentiation: Links to other terms

Year 4, Term 3: Y4T3SL4 to recognise how commas are used to join and separate clauses; to identify in their writing where each is more effective.

- Identify the clauses separated by a comma, for example, *They smell rotten, my feet*. Ask the children to identify which part of the sentence is a clause (*they smell rotten*) and which is a phrase (*my feet*). Explain to the children that they can tell which part is a clause because the clause contains the verb and makes sense on its own.

> I have been here before,
> But when or how I cannot tell:
> I know the grass beyond the door,
> The sweet keen smell,
> The sighing sound, the lights around the shore.
>
> Dante Gabriel Rossetti
> (Sudden Light)

The Wise Young Owl

by Philip Burton

Term 3

Range: Poetry that plays with language.

Introduction

Read the title with the children. In what way is the title unexpected? What would they normally expect? Are wise owls usually young or old? Now read the poem. Does it make sense to the children?

Text level work

- Y3T3TL6 to compare forms or types of humour, e.g. by exploring, collecting and categorising form or type of humour, e.g. nonsense verse.
- Y3T3TL7 to select, prepare, read aloud and recite by heart poetry that plays with language or entertains; to recognise rhyme, **alliteration** and other patterns of sound that create effects.

Teaching strategies

- Compare *The Wise Young Owl* with *Crescent Moon* and *Moonwatcher*, both by Sue Cowling. Identify the different types of poems.

- Inform the children that this is a **narrative** poem.

- Discuss the main sequence of events that takes place and the characters.

- Identify the narrative as imaginary nonsense, but nonsense that might hide a deeper meaning.

- The poet uses **simile** to describe the stars as beads. Ensure the children understand the use of simile as 'imaginative substitution'. Remind the children that a simile is the same as a **metaphor** (words which describe something by relating it to something else with which it has no realistic connection) but that it uses the term 'like' to link the comparison.

- Construct a list of other things that might be found in the sky that Kylie could give to the owl, and provide some suitable similes or metaphors, such as 'cushions like clouds' or 'a scarf like snowflakes'.

- Discuss the rhyme pattern. (It is abcb defe ghih.) The rhyming words are *moon* and *soon*, *beads* and *displeased*, *tat* and *that*.)

- Discuss the last words spoken by the owl. Check the children's understanding of these words.

Questions to ask

- How are these poems the same? (They are all fantastical in content.)
  How are they different? (*The Wise Young Owl* has no shaping in the text.)

- What is the story of the poem? Who are the main characters? What does Kylie do? What does the owl do?

- Is it possible to break the moon or thread stars like beads? Does the poet want to convey a message? What is his message?

- What are similes? What picture does the poet create by using similes? How many different similes are used in the poem? What about metaphors – can you remember how they are different?

- What else might Kylie give to the owl from the sky? Can you invent some different similes or metaphors for those things?

- Which lines of verse rhyme? List the rhyming words.

- Why was the owl displeased with Kylie? How does the owl correct Kylie's actions?

Sentence level work

- Y3T3SL7 to become aware of the use of commas in marking grammatical boundaries within sentences.
- Y3T3SL4 to use speech marks and other dialogue punctuation appropriately in writing and to use the conventions which mark boundaries between spoken words and the rest of the sentence.

Teaching strategies

- Identify the commas in *The Wise Young Owl* and why they are used (to denote speech and to create pauses in the sentences).
- Identify which words are usually written as direct speech. Put in the speech marks around the dialogue. (The italics are the direct speech.)
- Discuss reasons why the poet has not used speech marks.

Questions to ask

- *When has the poet used commas? Why has he used them there?*
- *Which words are spoken? Where should we put the speech marks?*
- *Why do you think the poet has used italics instead of speech marks?* (It gives more emphasis to the owl – who is right.)

Word level work

- Y3T3WL12 to continue the collection of new words from reading and work in other subjects, and making use of them in reading and writing.
- Y3T3WL16 to collect, investigate, classify common expressions from reading and own experience.

Teaching strategies

- Collect any unfamiliar words or expressions in the poem, for example, *utterly displeased*. Ask the children to find out the meaning of these expressions.
- Investigate ways to express warnings or corrections on the same lines as *That's that*, for example, 'That's not so bright'.
- Collect some more ideas for expressions the owl might say as a reprimand or warning.

Questions to ask

- *Are any of the words in the poem new to you? What do you think they mean? Are you right?*
- *Which words does the owl use to correct Kylie? Can you think of any similar expressions?*
- *What would you say to Kylie to warn her to stop? Which different expressions could you use?*

Differentiation: Links to other terms

Year 5, Term 2: Y5T2TL10 to understand the differences between literal and figurative language, e.g. through discussing the effects of imagery in poetry and prose.

- Look again at the phrase *and threaded stars like beads*. Do the children think it is a good simile? How does the poet take his simile a step further? (The stars actually become a necklace.) Compare this with the use of simile in *Nature Shapes* by Sue Cowling. Compare the differences between simile and metaphor.

- Discuss the wider effect of the simile *and threaded stars like beads*. The simile reinforces the idea of the ease with which Kylie does these incredible things. Discuss the fact that although Kylie can perform these feats very easily, it is more difficult to make the correct decisions, as the owl does.

Term 3

A Shaggy Dog Story
by Marian Swinger

Range

Poetry that plays with language.

Introduction

Discuss the title with the children. Do they know what a shaggy dog story is? Have they ever heard a shaggy dog story? Can they retell the story? Do they expect to believe a shaggy dog story?

Text level work

- Y3T3TL6 to compare forms or types of humour, e.g. by exploring, collecting and categorising form or type of humour, e.g. nonsense verse.

Teaching strategies

- Read the poem through once with the children. Discuss the impossibility of the journeys that the dog makes.

- Discuss the rhyme pattern of the four-line verse. (It is abcb defe ghih.)

- Identify the rhyming words. (*sea* and *tea*, *aeroplane* and *again*, *car* and *star*.)

- Note the rhyme contained in the last verse, *tiny shiny car*.

- Note the **alliteration** in *the wild and windy sea*.

- Construct different journeys for the shaggy dog story in shared writing, for example:

    A shaggy dog went riding
    Across the Texas plain.
    He rode ten thousand metres
    And then rode home again

- Illustrate the children's different verses.

- Ask the children to tell each other shaggy dog stories, working in pairs. The stories should be as fantastical as possible.

- Make a class book of shaggy dog stories and poems. Select stories which could be rewritten as poems.

Questions to ask

- *Where did the shaggy dog go? Are the dog's journeys possible? Which journey is most incredible? Why do you think that? What are the different forms of transport he used? Which is your favourite verse? Why?*

- *What is the rhyme pattern of the poem? Which lines of verse do you think are most effective? Why?*

- *Can you add your own verse to describe a different shaggy dog journey? Can you suggest any other activities for the dog to try, like skiing or swimming?*

- *Can you tell your own shaggy dog story?*

The more I see of men, the better I like dogs.

Attributed to Mme Roland

Glossary

I am very grateful to John Turner of Sheffield Hallam University for his assistance in compiling parts of this glossary.

acrostic
a poem in which the first letters of each line read down to make a word, linked to the poem's meaning

alliteration
the use of words that contain the same letters to create an effect

assonance
the rhyming, or near rhyming, of similar vowel sounds in a poem

cadence
the beat of something rhythmical

caesura
a pause or break in the middle of a line

calligram
a poem in which the shape of the letters fits the poem's meaning

chorus – see repeating refrain

concrete poem
a poem where the physical shape and design of the poem contributes strongly to its meaning

couplet
a pair of lines

end-stopped rhyme (end-stop)
the common form of rhyme where similar sounds are repeated at the end of a line and the natural sense of the line stops at that point

enjambement (run-on line)
when the natural sense of the line runs into the next without a grammatical break

eye-rhyme
where words rhyme by sight and not by sound, e.g. 'though' and 'plough'

free verse
poetry that relies on the rhythms of natural speech for its effect. It may or may not be in regular stanzas. It moves away from regular, metrical form.

half-rhyme
where line endings consist of words that have the same terminal consonant sounds but different vowel sounds. True rhyme is almost achieved.

internal rhyme
rhymes occurring inside the same line

list poem
a simple poem with short lines, each one of which makes natural sense and then stops

metaphor
a thing is spoken of as being that which it resembles, such as 'the storm is a lion', 'the ferocious swan a tiger'

metrical pattern
the pattern of metre, the overall sound pattern of the poem, its regular system of stressed and unstressed syllables

narrative
the story a poem tells

near rhyme
a broad term meaning half-rhyme

non-rhyming couplet
a pair of lines that do not rhyme with each other

onomatopoeia
the use of words that sound like their meaning

performance poem
a poem that suits being performed

pictogram
a symbol which is used to represent a word, or words, as in Chinese writing

portmanteau word
a word that contains the sense and sound of two words

refrain
a repeated motif, line or chorus

regular rhyme
when the rhyming pattern of a poem is constant and predictable

repeating refrain (chorus)
a section of the poem that repeats, often between verses

rhyming couplet
when a pair of lines rhyme

run-on line
see enjambement

scansion
the analysis of a poem according to its metrical measure

shape poem
a poem that is laid out or drawn to look like its meaning

simile
a comparison usually using the words 'like' or 'as'

synonym
a word that means the same, or nearly the same, as another word